W9-BLO-021

# MINI ENCYCLOPEDIA

# BIRDS

### Authors
Barbara Taylor
Jinny Johnson

# Miles Kelly

First published as *Birds* in 2010 by Miles Kelly Publishing Ltd
Harding's Barn, Bardfield End Green, Thaxted, Essex, CM6 3PX, UK

Copyright © Miles Kelly Publishing Ltd 2010

This edition printed 05/14

LOT#:
2 4 6 8 10 9 7 5 3 1

**Publishing Director** Belinda Gallagher
**Creative Director** Jo Cowan
**Managing Editor** Rosie Neave
**Editor** Sarah Parkin
**Assistant Editor** Claire Philip
**Cover Designer** Jo Cowan
**Series Designer** Helen Bracey
**Volume Designer** Rocket Design Ltd
**Junior Designer** Kayleigh Allen
**Image Manager** Liberty Newton
**Indexer** Indexing Specialists (UK) Ltd
**Production Manager** Elizabeth Collins
**Reprographics** Stephan Davis, Simon Lee, Jennifer Cozens
**Assets** Lorraine King

ISBN 978-1-4351-5639-5

Printed in China

British Library Cataloguing-in-Publication Data
A catalogue record for this book is available from the British Library

Made with paper from a sustainable forest

www.mileskelly.net
info@mileskelly.net

# Contents

 ## What is a bird?

## How birds live

# Bird habitats

# Perching birds

# Birds of prey and owls

# Waders and water birds

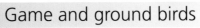

# Game and ground birds

# Woodland and forest birds

# People and birds

# What is a bird?

# The world of birds

- **There are more than 10,000** species of birds.

- **Scientists estimate** that there are about 300 billion individual birds in the world—that's 50 birds for every person on the planet.

- **More than a third** of all known bird species live and breed in South and Central America.

- **All birds** lay hard-shelled eggs, in which their young develop. If a mother bird had young that developed inside her body instead, she would be too heavy to fly.

- **One of the most widespread** of all birds is the osprey, which is found nearly all over the world.

- **The marsh warbler** is one of the greatest mimics of the bird world, able to imitate the songs of more than 70 different species.

- **The world's heaviest flying birds** are the kori bustard and the great bustard, which weigh up to 40 lb.

- **The wandering albatross** is one of the longest-lived birds. Individuals may live as long as 60 years or more.

- **The red-billed quelea** is probably the most common wild bird. There are thought to be at least 1.5 billion.

- **The largest bird**, the ostrich, weighs almost 80,000 times more than the smallest, the bee hummingbird.

▶ *Many birds are highly sociable, flocking together to feed and raise their young.*

# Bird groups

- **A species** is a particular type of bird. Birds of the same species can mate and have young, and these can themselves have offspring.

- **The 10,000 bird species** are organized into about 200 families. Species in a family share certain characteristics, such as body shape.

- **Bird families** are organized into about 30 larger groups called orders. Largest is the perching bird order, with more species than all the other bird orders put together.

- **There are over 70 different family groups** in the perching bird order, Passeriformes.

## How is a barn owl classified?

| | |
|---|---|
| **KINGDOM** | Animalia (animals) |
| **PHYLUM** | Chordata (animals with spinal cords) |
| **SUBPHYLUM** | Vertebrata (animals with backbones) |
| **CLASS** | Aves (birds) |
| **SUBCLASS** | Neornithes (all birds except *Archaeopteryx*) |
| **ORDER** | Strigiformes (all owls) |
| **FAMILY** | Tytonidae (barn owls) |
| **GENUS** | *Tyto* |
| **SPECIES** | *Tyto alba* |

▲ Scientists classify animals, such as birds, into a series of increasingly narrow categories, based on features they have in common. The largest category is the entire animal kingdom, the smallest category is an individual species of bird.

- **The study of birds** is known as ornithology, which comes from two Greek words, *ornithos*, meaning "bird" and *logos*, meaning "knowledge."

**DID YOU KNOW?**
The scientific system for classifying (grouping) all living things, including birds, was thought up by a Swedish naturalist, called Linnaeus, in the 18th century.

- **Scientists called taxonomists** give scientific names to individual birds. These names are in Latin and each one includes a genus and a species name, such as *Passer domesticus* for the house sparrow.

- **The large flightless birds,** such as the ostrich and emu, in the Struthioniformes order are sometimes called ratites. Their name comes from the Latin *ratis*, meaning "raft." because they have a flat breastbone, without a raised keel for the attachment of flight muscles.

- **There is a lot of debate** about bird classification and scientists keep revising the classification system as new information from DNA analysis, molecular data, or fossils comes to light.

- **Separating one bird species** into two or more new species is called "splitting" and combining two species into one new species is called "lumping."

- **Modern birds** are divided into two superorders: Paleognathae (ostriches, emus, and relatives, as well as tinamous) and Neognathae (all other birds).

# Water birds

- **Sphenisciformes** (penguins) are flightless seabirds, which live in the Southern Hemisphere. They have dense, waterproof feathers and webbed feet.

- **Gaviiformes** (divers) are large, diving waterbirds, with long, straight bills for catching fish. Their legs are set far back on their bodies, which is good for diving but makes it difficult for them to walk on land.

- **Podicipediformes** (grebes) are small-to-medium-sized diving waterbirds with chisel-like bills, lobed feet, and dense feathers. These birds make floating nests.

- **Procellariiformes** (shearwaters, petrels, and albatrosses) are seabirds that fly well. They have hooked bills and a well-developed sense of smell.

- **Pelecaniformes** (pelicans, cormorants, gannets, and boobies) are seabirds with short legs, four webbed toes, and long wings.

- **Ciconiiformes** (herons, egrets, ibises, and storks) have long legs and long necks. They feed by wading in shallow water and often breed in large colonies.

▼ *Penguins spend most of their lives in the water, coming onto land or sea ice only to lay eggs and raise their young. These are emperor penguins, which are the biggest penguins in the world.*

▲ *Flamingos live and breed in noisy colonies in shallow lakes, sometimes forming flocks containing thousands, or even a million, birds.*

 **Phoenicopteriformes** (flamingos) have long legs, webbed front toes, and long necks. They feed by filtering food through a unique curved bill.

 **Anseriformes** (ducks, swans, and geese) have short legs, webbed feet, and fluffy young. Most have a flat, wide, rounded bill.

 **Gruiformes** (cranes, rails, and coots) are a diverse group, which fly with their necks held straight out. Many are shy birds that are not often seen.

 **Charadriiformes** (shorebirds, gulls, terns, and auks) is a large and mixed group of about 16 families, which are often associated with shoreline habitats.

◀ *Mute swans have a distinctive orange bill. They are graceful birds that originally came from central Asia, but now live all over the world on parkland lakes and slow-moving waters.*

17

# Land birds

- **Tinamiformes** (tinamous) are flying birds with four toes and chickenlike bills. They live only in Central and South America.

- **Casuariidae** (cassowaries) are flightless birds found in Australia, Papua New Guinea, and eastern Indonesia. They have three toes and a casque (bony extension) on the top of their heads.

- **Falconiformes** (eagles, hawks, and falcons) are diurnal (day-active) birds of prey with hooked bills, curved talons (claws), and strong wings.

- **Stringiformes** (owls) are nocturnal (night-active) predators, with a round head, forward-facing eyes, keen hearing, a hooked bill, and sharp talons.

- **Galliformes** (turkey, grouse, quail, and pheasant) have strong legs, which are well-developed for walking. Their wings are short and rounded, and the bill is short and downcurved, with an overlapping tip.

- **Psittaciformes** (parrots, lories, and macaws) have a large head with a heavy, hooked bill. Their strong feet have two toes facing forward and two backward for perching and climbing.

- **Coliformes** (mousebirds) are small African birds with crests on their heads and long tails.

◄ Kestrels hover in the air as they search for prey, such as small mammals, on the ground below. They are often seen hovering beside busy roads.

**Apodiformes** (swifts and hummingbirds) are small birds with short legs and weak feet. They are extremely good at flying.

**Coraciiformes** (kingfishers and rollers) are chunky birds with large heads and thick bills. Many are brightly colored, noisy birds that live in groups.

**Piciformes** (woodpeckers) have barb-tipped tongues, stiffened tail feathers, and feet with two toes pointing back and two forward. They drill into wood with their beaks to look for food or make nest holes.

▶ Emus are large, flightless, Australian birds, which wander up to 600 mi a year across the Australian outback. They have powerful legs and are most closely related to cassowaries.

# Early birds

- **The oldest-known feathers** of any creature belong to a small feathered dinosaur called *Anchiornis huxleyi*, which lived in China between 150 and 160 million years ago.

- **Scientists believe** that birds evolved from lightly built dinosaurs, such as *Compsognathus*, which ran on two legs.

- **The earliest-known bird** is *Archaeopteryx*, which lived 155 to 150 million years ago. It had feathers like a modern bird, but teeth like a reptile.

- **Although it could fly**, *Archaeopteryx* could not take off from the ground, and probably had to climb a tree before launching itself into the air.

◀ *Archaeopteryx was about the size of a crow, with a wingspan of 24 in. Its name means "ancient wing."*

▶ Titanis walleri *lived in North and South America from five to two million years ago. Its skull was about 20 in long and it was up to 8 ft tall. Its small wings could not have been used for flying.*

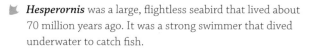

*Ichthyornis* was a seabird with long, toothed jaws. It lived alongside dinosaurs in the Late Cretaceous period.

*Ichthyornis* is the oldest known bird to have a narrow ridge (keel) on its breastbone for the attachment of the large chest muscles that powered its wings.

*Hesperornis* was a large, flightless seabird that lived about 70 million years ago. It was a strong swimmer that dived underwater to catch fish.

**The ancient flightless bird** *Diatryma* lived in North America and Europe about 50 million years ago. It stood about 6.5 ft tall on its long legs and probably used its hooked beak to catch mammals.

**The largest-known** predatory bird to have ever lived is a terror bird, *Titanis walleri*. It died out from two to one million years ago. This flightless bird could run after prey at speeds of up to 40 mph and used its large claws and sharp bill to make the kill.

**DID YOU KNOW?**

Dinosaurs probably used feathers for display for millions of years, before some evolved into birds and used them for flying.

**An early member** of the vulture family, *Argentavix* of South America had an amazing 24 ft wingspan.

21

# Extinct birds

**Scientists estimate** that over 150 bird species have probably become extinct since the year 1500, largely because of hunting and the introduction of mammals, such as rats, cats, pigs, and dogs, which eat their eggs and young.

**There were once** about 20 species of flightless moas living in New Zealand, but most of them became extinct before 1400; a few survived into the 1600s.

**Haast's eagle**—the world's largest-known eagle—preyed on moas and died out when they became extinct. It attacked at speeds of up to 50 mph, seizing prey in its giant talons.

**The New Zealand quail** became extinct in about 1875 after extensive hunting for sport and food by European settlers, and the destruction of its grassland habitat.

**The great auk** lived on Earth for millions of years, but became extinct in the mid-19th century after being hunted for its fat, which was burned in oil lamps.

◀ The great auk was up to 34 in tall and developed a white patch over the eye during the breeding season. This flightless seabird dived underwater to catch food, rather like a penguin.

► The dodo's small, stubby wings were no use for flying. These large birds were related to pigeons and used their hooked beaks to eat fruits and seeds. They only laid one egg at a time, on the ground.

- **Dodos were flightless birds** the size of large turkeys. They were hunted to extinction by people and introduced predators, such as pigs and rats. They were curious, clumsy, slow-moving birds that were easy to catch.

- **Passenger pigeons** were once the most common birds in North America. Total populations may have reached five billion individuals and flocks were so dense that they darkened the sky. They were wiped out in the wild by 1900, due to overhunting by European settlers and habitat destruction.

- *Aepyornis* **(also known as the "elephant bird")**, a 10-ft-tall ostrich ancestor from Madagascar, probably became extinct in the 17th century.

- **The eggs** of *Aepyornis* may have weighed as much as 22 lb—more than nine times the weight of an ostrich egg today.

# Record-breaking birds

- **The bald eagle** builds the largest nest of any bird. One nest can weigh as much as two army jeeps.

- **Emperor penguins** can dive to depths of over 1,300 ft, although most of their dives are less than 330 ft.

- **The wandering albatross** has the largest wingspan of any bird alive today, measuring up to 11.5 ft. It also has 88 flight feathers—more than any other bird.

- **The ostrich** lays the largest egg of any living bird. The egg is equal in volume to 24 chicken's eggs and the shell is so strong it can support the weight of a person.

- **The bee hummingbird** lays the smallest egg of any living bird. The egg is only 6 mm long and about the size of a pea.

▼ The bald eagle's huge nest is a platform of sticks called an eyrie, which is built high in a tree.

▲ Some peregrines fly up to 15,500 mi a year—the name "peregrine" means "wanderer." Swifts fly up to 19,500 ft high and drink by catching raindrops as they fly.

- **The roadrunner** is the fastest runner of all the flying birds. It dashes across the deserts of North America at speeds of up to 23 mph.

- **The biggest bird bill** in the world belongs to the Australian pelican. It grows up to 18.5 in long.

- **The common swift** spends more time in the air than any other land bird. It remains in the air for up to three years, even sleeping on the wing.

- **The female gray partridge** is the bird that lays the most eggs at any one time—as many as 15–19 eggs in just one clutch.

- **The peregrine** (a type of falcon) is the fastest bird, diving through the air at 112 mph to catch prey.

▶ The Australian pelican is the largest of the eight pelican species. The very large bill pouch holds 2–3.5 gal of water and is used for catching fish.

# The structure of birds

- **Birds are the only animals** to have feathers. These keep them warm and protected from the weather and, in most species, allow them to fly.

- **Like mammals**, fish, and reptiles, birds are vertebrate animals— this means that they have backbones.

- **Birds have a body temperature** of between 104°F and 111.2°F— higher than other warm-blooded animals.

- **Birds have a lightweight beak**, or bill, made of bone covered by layers of a substance called keratin. This same substance makes up human hair and fingernails.

- **Birds do not have teeth** inside their bills, so they cannot chew their food. Some birds, such as birds of prey, use their bills to tear up their food.

- **A bird's feathers** and claws are also made of keratin.

- **Birds do not have true tails** with bones down the middle. Their tail feathers are attached to a bony stump called the pygostyle.

- **Birds have** a very high metabolic rate, which is the rate at which they can burn up food and release the energy it contains. This creates the energy they need for flight.

**DID YOU KNOW**

A bird looks as if its knees bend backward, but this joint is in fact the ankle joint, so birds walk on their toes. A bird's knees are higher up its legs, hidden under its feathers.

🪶 **Birds have mobile necks**, so they can look all around for danger or food.

🪶 **A bird's ears and knees** are hidden under its feathers.

▶ *The main external parts of a bird are shown on this mistle thrush.*

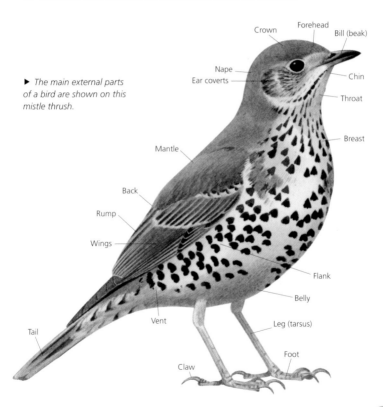

Crown

Forehead

Bill (beak)

Nape

Ear coverts

Chin

Throat

Breast

Mantle

Back

Rump

Wings

Flank

Belly

Vent

Leg (tarsus)

Tail

Foot

Claw

27

# Bones and muscles

- **Bird bones** have a honeycomb structure. They are so light that they account for only about 5 percent of a bird's total weight.

- **Birds' muscles** make up 30–60 percent of their total weight. The biggest are the flight and leg muscles.

- **Small birds** have about 15 neck vertebrae, while the mute swan has 23. Mammals have only seven.

- **The skeleton** of a bird's wings has a similar structure to the human arm, but the wrist bones are joined. Also, a bird has much reduced bones for three fingers, not five fingers like us.

- **The breastbone** of a flying bird has a large ridge, or keel, providing a surface to which the flight muscles can be anchored.

- **A bird's wishbone** is made up of its two collarbones joined together. As the powerful wing muscles pull downward, the wishbone helps to keep the wing joint in position so the bird's body is not crushed.

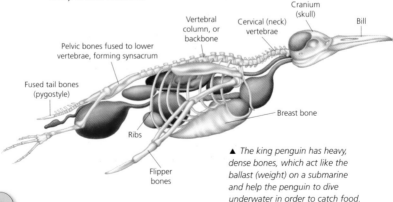

Cranium (skull)

Vertebral column, or backbone

Cervical (neck) vertebrae

Bill

Pelvic bones fused to lower vertebrae, forming synsacrum

Fused tail bones (pygostyle)

Fused tail bones (pygostyle)

Breast bone

Ribs

Flipper bones

▲ The king penguin has heavy, dense bones, which act like the ballast (weight) on a submarine and help the penguin to dive underwater in order to catch food.

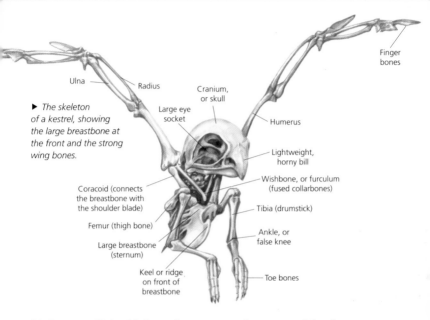

Ulna

Radius

Cranium, or skull

Large eye socket

Finger bones

Humerus

▶ The skeleton of a kestrel, showing the large breastbone at the front and the strong wing bones.

Lightweight, horny bill

Wishbone, or furculum (fused collarbones)

Coracoid (connects the breastbone with the shoulder blade)

Femur (thigh bone)

Tibia (drumstick)

Ankle, or false knee

Large breastbone (sternum)

Keel or ridge on front of breastbone

Toe bones

- **In many diving birds**, such as penguins, bones are solid and heavy. This makes it easier for these birds to dive under the water.

- **The bones of flightless birds** are also solid because they do not need lightweight skeletons for flight.

- **The main bulk** of the wing muscles are at the base of the wing, close to the bird's center of gravity. The leg muscles are near the top of the leg for the same reason.

- **Birds have** a smaller number of bones than we do because many of their bones (such as the two lower leg bones) are fused together. Birds have about 112 bones (the number varies in different species), whereas all humans have 206 bones in their skeleton.

# How birds work

- **Birds do not** have teeth. Instead their food is ground down by a part of the digestive system called the gizzard. Some birds swallow small stones to help the action of the gizzard.

- **Up to one fifth** of a bird's body is taken up by large air sacs, which are at the base of the neck, within the chest cavity and in the abdomen.

▼ *The main internal organs of a pigeon, showing the large crop and gizzard, which is the last pocket in a bird's stomach.*

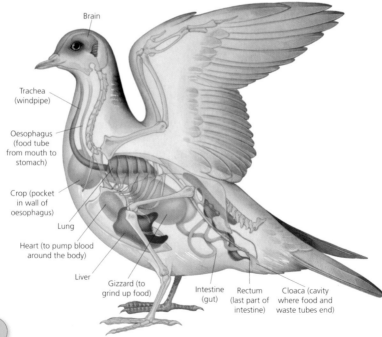

Brain

Trachea (windpipe)

Oesophagus (food tube from mouth to stomach)

Crop (pocket in wall of oesophagus)

Lung

Heart (to pump blood around the body)

Liver

Gizzard (to grind up food)

Intestine (gut)

Rectum (last part of intestine)

Cloaca (cavity where food and waste tubes end)

- **A bird's air sacs** are connected to its lungs and even extend into the wing bones.

- **The air in the air sacs** helps to make a bird lighter and also cools its body down. This is important because birds have no sweat glands and cannot cool the body by perspiring.

- **When a bird breathes**, air passes through its lungs twice, allowing it to get as much oxygen as possible out of each breath. This makes its lungs very efficient.

- **Some birds**, such as finches and pigeons, have a storage chamber called a crop at the side of their gullet. They can cram a lot of food into the crop in a short time, then retire to a safe place to eat it. Many birds use the crop to carry food back to their young in the nest.

- **Birds do not** have a bladder to collect waste water, which makes their bodies more lightweight. Instead, they remove most of the water from their food in the gut before they excrete very concentrated wastes, which are made mostly of uric acid.

- **Penguins are able** to drink sea water because they have special glands in their bills that help to get rid of extra salt from their blood. The glands produce a salty liquid, which drips out of the nose.

- **Penguins have** a thick layer of fatty blubber under the skin, which stops body heat from leaking out and keeps the birds warm. The blubber works rather like an insulated jacket.

- **The heart rate** of a tiny hummingbird reaches an astonishing 615 beats a minute when in mid flight.

# Beaks

- **A beak** is made up of a bird's projecting jaw bones, covered in a hard horny material called keratin.

- **The hyacinth macaw** has one of the most powerful beaks of any bird, strong enough to crack Brazil nuts.

- **Nightjars** have the shortest beaks, at 8–10 mm long.

- **A bird's beak** is extremely sensitive to touch. Birds that probe in the ground for food have extra sensory organs at the beak tip.

- **Red-breasted mergansers** have serrated (jagged) edges to their beaks, like the teeth on the blade of a saw. This helps them to get a firm grip on slippery fish.

▶ *The hooked beak of the gyrfalcon is typical of a bird of prey. It uses its sharp beak to tear up its prey, which includes rodents, hares, ducks, and even owls. The gyrfalcon is the largest and most powerful of the falcons.*

▶ The crossbill is so-called because the upper and lower portions of its beak cross over one another.

🐦 **The puffin** has special spines on the upper part of its beak and its tongue. This enables it to carry 50 or more sand eels in its bill at the same time.

🐦 **Seed-eating birds** have pyramid-shaped bills, which help them to crack open seeds. The Hawfinch can even crush cherry stones.

🐦 **A pelican** uses its huge, baggy bill pouch to scoop up fish from the water, rather like a fishing net.

🐦 **A dagger-shaped bill** is characteristic of fish-eating birds, such as herons and kingfishers.

🐦 **Birds that feed on insects**, such as bee-eaters, have thin, pointed bills to probe under bark and stones.

**DID YOU KNOW?**

A baby bird has a spike called an "egg tooth" on its beak for breaking its way out of its egg.

33

# Legs and feet

- **A bird's legs and feet** are covered in scales, a link to the ancient ancestors of birds, the scale-covered reptiles.

- **Coots and grebes** have lobes of scaly skin growing between their toes. These act as paddles in the water and also stop them sinking into the mud on marshy ground.

- **The feathers** on the legs and feet of most owls help them to swoop down silently on their prey.

- **Birds of prey** have long, curved talons on their toes for catching and killing their prey. Most birds of prey find it difficult to walk on their talons.

- **On land**, small birds use their legs to hop, while larger birds use their legs for walking.

- **Wading birds**, or shorebirds, such as sandpipers and curlews, have long legs for walking through water in search of food. Storks and herons have long legs for the same reason.

▼ The barn owl has strong, feathered legs with pointed, curled talons for killing and carrying prey.

▼ The black vulture has broad feet for walking, but its claws are flat because it feeds on dead animals and does not need them for killing.

► *The ostrich is the only bird to have two toes on each foot. Emu, rheas, and cassowaries have three toes and most other birds have four toes.*

🪶 **Four-toed birds** have different arrangements of toes: in swifts, all four point forward; in most perching birds, three point forward and one backward; in owls and woodpeckers, two point forward and two point backward.

🪶 **An owl's first and fourth toes** usually point backward, but the fourth toe can be rotated to the front, to help hold food and grab prey.

🪶 **Webbed feet** make all waterbirds very efficient paddlers.

🪶 **The second and third toes** of kingfishers are fused together to help them swim underwater to catch fish.

▼ *Penguins use their webbed feet for steering and braking as they swim underwater. Their thick, strong claws help them to grip slippery rocks and icy surfaces when they walk on land.*

Gentoo penguin          Rockhopper penguin          Jackass penguin

# Feathers

🪶 **Feathers evolved** from reptile scales and they grow out of little pits, or follicles, in a bird's skin, just as the hairs on human skin grow from hair follicles.

🪶 **Feathers grow** at a rate of 1–13 mm a day.

🪶 **The ruby-throated hummingbird** has only 940 feathers, while the whistling swan has 25,216.

🪶 **A bird's feathers** are replaced once or twice a year in a process known as "molting."

🪶 **Feathers keep a bird warm**, protect its skin, provide a flight surface, and may also attract a mate.

▶ An anhinga preening its feathers.

**DID YOU KNOW?**
The male crested argus pheasant has the longest and largest tail feathers, which are 68 in long and 5 in wide.

▼ Flight feathers on a bird's wings and tail provide a large continuous surface area to push the bird through the air. Their airfoil shape helps to lift the bird into the air as well as twist and turn in flight.

▼ Soft down feathers trap warm air next to a bird's body. The side branches (barbs) are long and soft. There are few hooks (barbules) to hold the barbs together, so the feather stays fluffy.

▼ Body, or contour, feathers overlap like tiles on a roof, to keep the bird's body warm and dry. The inner part of a body feather is fluffy, like a down feather.

🪶 **In most birds**, a third of the feathers are on the head.

🪶 **The longest feathers** ever known were 34.75 ft long and belonged to an ornamental chicken.

🪶 **The feathers** that cover a bird's body are called contour feathers. Down feathers underneath provide extra warmth.

🪶 **The 7,182 feathers** of a bald eagle weigh 1,493 lb, more than twice as much as the bird's skeleton.

🪶 **Birds spend time** every day "preening"—cleaning and rearranging their feathers with their beaks.

# Flight

- **Most birds** can fly and they are the largest, fastest, and most powerful flying animals on the planet.

- **Flight** allows birds to escape danger, exploit different food sources, and migrate to warmer places for the winter.

- **A flying bird's wings** are an airfoil shape—slightly curved on top and hollow underneath. This shape makes the air flow faster over the top of the wings than underneath, creating lower pressure above the wing and lifting the bird up into the air.

- **Some birds**, such as birds of prey, can soar upward by hitching a lift on rising currents of hot air, called thermals.

- **Many birds** have a flapping method of flying. As they flap their wings down, they push the air down and back, which thrusts the bird forward and upward.

▼ *Large birds of prey, such as eagles or vultures, use rising currents of hot air (thermals) to lift them up to great heights. They spread their wings wide and circle higher and higher into the sky.*

As ground air is heated, it becomes lighter

Lighter, warmer air rises, creating thermals

Thermals help big birds fly and soar

▶ Owls have fluffy, comblike fringes on their wing feathers, which have a soft, velvety surface. This muffles the sound of their wing beats so they can swoop silently down onto their prey.

**Many birds** shut their wings for short rests during a period of flapping flight. This helps them to save energy.

**Most birds** beat their wings at between three and eight times a second during flapping flight, but herons only flap their wings at two or three times a second.

**A few birds**, such as hummingbirds and kestrels, are able to hover in the air, but this uses up a huge amount of energy. A kestrel flies into the wind at the same speed as the wind blowing against it, but has to work hard to hover over one spot as it watches for its prey on the ground below.

**Smaller birds** take off by jumping up into the air and flapping their wings. A heavy bird, such as a swan, has to run along while flapping its wings to generate enough lift for takeoff. A swan may need to run 160 ft or more to get into the air.

**When birds land**, they spread out their wings and tail like brakes. Heavy birds land into the wind to help themselves slow down.

# Flightless birds

- **A few birds** have given up flying altogether, either because they are too heavy to fly or because they don't need to fly to survive.

- **Many flightless birds**, such as ostriches or emus, are very large birds that can run much faster than their enemies. Emus can travel long distances on land to search for food without becoming tired.

- **Large, flightless birds** have strong legs and claws and can deliver a vicious kick if an enemy gets too close.

- **Some birds** lost the power of flight because they lived on remote islands where there were few natural enemies.

▼ *A flightless cormorant spreads out its stubby wings after swimming in the sea near the Galápagos Islands, which are west of South America in the Pacific Ocean.*

▶ The kakapo is a rare nocturnal parrot from New Zealand, which lives on the ground and cannot fly. Its green feathers provide good camouflage in its forest home.

- **Many types** of flightless rail have evolved on remote islands. They have slim bodies, which allow them to move quickly through thick undergrowth and hide from danger.

- **Wekas** are large flightless rails from New Zealand with powerful bills and feet. They often raid garbage and are fierce predators of other birds that live on the ground.

- **Flightless birds** on islands have no means of escape from people or the predators, such as cats and rats, which people introduce to the islands.

- **The flightless Galápagos cormorant** uses its small, weak wings to shade its chicks from the hot sun and to help it to balance on land.

- **Penguins** are such expert swimmers that they do not need to fly. Their wings have become flippers to help them "fly" underwater, using their tail like a rudder to change direction. A penguin's wings cannot be folded up like the wings of most birds.

- **The flightless** Magellanic steamer ducks of South America are named after their habit of furiously paddling over the water, "steaming" on their stubby wings to escape predators.

41

# Wings and tails

**Black-thighed falconet**

*◀ The shape of a bird's wings is suited to the way it flies. A falconet has narrow, pointed wings for rapid wing beats and fast flight. A buzzard has long, wide wings to soar high in the sky without flapping its wings.*

**Common buzzard**

🦅 **A bird's wings** are modified arms. Inside a bird's wing are the same sort of bones as there are in the human arm, but highly modified. We have 29 bones in our arms, while a pigeon has only 11 such bones.

🦅 **Many large birds,** such as eagles, buzzards, and pelicans, have slotted wingtips that spread apart like fingers. This allows the wing tips to be adjusted to reduce drag, increase lift, and create a more stable flight.

🦅 **Fast-flying birds,** such as swifts and falcons, have long, flat, narrow, triangular wings, which are swept backward like the wings of a high-speed jet fighter.

🦅 **Hummingbirds** rotate their wings at the shoulder, not at the wrist, as most other birds do. This allows their wings to be turned over in mid-stroke.

🦅 **Swans** are the second-heaviest flying birds in the world. Their wings are each nearly 24 in long.

🦅 **Most of a bird's tail** is made up of feathers—about 12 of them.

🦅 **Birds use their tails** for flight, perching, balance, or attracting the attention of a mate.

▲ *The long tail feathers of the male peacock are very impressive when spread out to attract a female (peahen). As part of its display, the peacock shakes its tail feathers, making the false "eyes" change color as they catch the light.*

**DID YOU KNOW?**

The wing feathers of large birds, such as geese and swans, can be made into quill pens by sharpening the tip into a nib that soaks up ink.

🐾 **A woodpecker** uses its stiff tail feathers for support as it climbs trees. The tips of the tail feathers wear down rapidly as they scrape against tree trunks.

🐾 **In some birds**, the outer tail feathers are the longest, giving the tail a forked shape. This gives the birds more maneuverability in the air.

🐾 **Some birds**, such as puffins, have hardly any tail feathers at all, while other birds, such as pheasants, peacocks, and birds of paradise, have long, colorful, and elaborate feathers that make flight quite difficult.

# How birds live

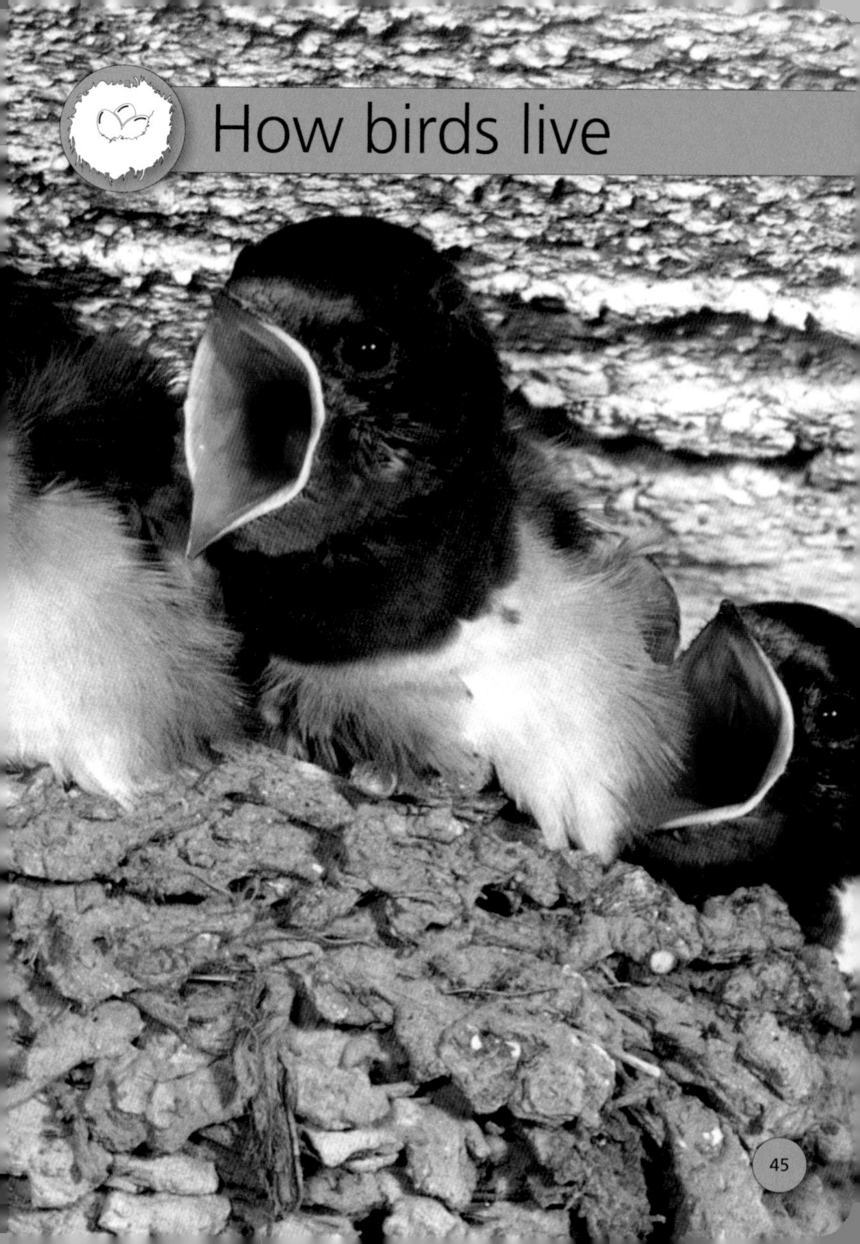

# Bird senses

- **Almost all birds** have excellent sight and most depend on their eyes for finding food.

- **A bird's outer ear** consists of a short tube leading from the eardrum to the outside. In most birds the ear openings are just behind the jaw.

- **A barn owl's hearing** is so good that it can detect and catch prey in complete darkness without using its eyes at all.

- **A chicken** has only 24 taste buds and a starling has about 200—a human has 9,000.

- **An eagle** can spot prey from as high as one mile above the ground.

- **A starling's eye** is as much as 15 percent of the total weight of its head. A human's eye is only one percent of the head weight.

▼ *Oilbirds live in caves and find their way through the darkness using a form of echolocation. They make clicking noises and listen for the echoes bouncing back from the walls and other objects, which tell them how far away things are.*

Nictitating membrane

▲ Owls' eyes face forward, helping them judge distance. Large pupils let more light fall onto the retina at the back of the eye, producing a clear image. As well as eyelids, owls have a special membrane that sweeps across the eye to clean and protect it.

**The diameter of an ostrich's eye** is 2 in. This is larger than any other land animal's eye.

**Birds** are ten times more sensitive to changes of pitch and intensity in sounds than humans.

**A bird's nostrils** are usually at the base of the beak, but in the kiwi, which has a better sense of smell than most birds, they are at the tip of the beak.

**Albatrosses** have a good sense of smell. In experiments, they have been attracted to food from a distance of 18 mi away.

▶ The tip of the snipe's bill is flexible and very sensitive, which allows it to detect and identify worms and other small creatures.

47

# Food and feeding

- **A few birds,** such as geese, ducks, and grouse, eat plants and leaves. This plant material is hard to digest and poor in nutrients, so the birds have to eat a lot of food to get the energy they need.

- **Hummingbirds and sunbirds** feed on the sweet nectar produced by flowers, which is rich in energy. The birds help to pollinate the flowers as they feed.

- **Some birds,** such as skuas and magpies, feed on the eggs and chicks of other birds.

- **Albatrosses** turn some of the squid and fish they catch into a high-energy oil, which they store in their stomachs. They feed this oil to their chicks, enabling the chicks to survive long periods without food while their parents are out at sea.

- **Some vultures** eat so much at one meal that they are too heavy to fly afterward.

- **Eagle owls** are very powerful predators, able to kill a mammal as large as a young deer.

◄ *A woodpecker uses its daggerlike bill to dig out nesting holes in tree trunks, and also to probe for insects under the tree bark.*

▲ *A flamingo filters food from the water with the sievelike fringes on the edge of its top bill. The bottom bill and the tongue move up and down to pump water through the bill fringes.*

**Birds in the crow family** eat almost anything, including insects, birds, mammals, worms, and seeds. They have a strong, multipurpose bill, which can cope well with all sorts of food.

**The woodpecker finch** uses twigs or cactus spines as tools to dig insect grubs out of crevices in tree bark.

**Birds digest their food** very quickly. Fruit takes only about 15 minutes to pass through their digestive systems. A bird such as a shrike takes only three hours to digest a mouse completely.

**Thrushes** smash snail shells against stones to break them open and then they feed on the snail inside.

# Color and camouflage

- **The colors** of a bird's feathers are usually produced either by colored pigments made inside the bird's body, or by the structure of the feathers and the way they reflect the light.

- **A peacock's feathers** are iridescent, which means they are shiny and shimmer with different colors as they move.

- **Some birds**, such as flamingos, get their colors from the food they eat.

- **Bird colors** help individuals of the same species to recognize each other.

- **Birds also use their colors** to attract a mate, threaten a rival, or camouflage themselves from predators.

- **Female birds** often have much duller plumage than male birds, so that they are camouflaged when they sit on their eggs.

- **The whip-poor-will** is rarely seen because it sleeps during the day on the forest floor. Its colors match the dead leaves, giving it perfect camouflage.

- **Male birds of paradise** open out their wings and tails to show off their astonishing colors in special displays to attract females.

- **Penguins** have a variety of colorful head crests and skin patterns that help them to recognize each other. They are also used for display and courtship.

- **Male and female** eclectus parrots are very different colors. The male bird is bright green, the female is red with a blue underside.

▶ *Toucans may use their large, brightly colored bills to attract mates, or to scare away predators or animals that compete with them for food. The keel-billed toucan is the national bird of Belize.*

## DID YOU KNOW?

The bright red North American cardinal is named after the red robes worn by Catholic cardinals.

# Attracting a mate

- **Many male birds**, including common terns and kingfishers, give the females a present of food as part of their courtship display. This shows that they will be able to provide food for their young.

- **Many birds nest in a territory**, choosing an area that has enough food for their young. Male birds sing in their territories to attract mates and to keep out rival males.

- **The great crested grebe** is best known for its amazing courtship dance, during which a male and female perform a series of movements in water and exchange pieces of weed.

- **Cranes** perform spectacular courtship dances that involve a pair of birds leaping in the air, bowing, and flapping their wings.

- **Little auks** have a special courtship flight, in which the position of their wings and the speed at which they beat them are different from their normal flight.

▼ During courtship, a male heron (right) stretches its long neck up into the air and then lowers it over its back. Male and female herons make a variety of noisy calls and bill-clapping sounds while courting.

▲ *A great crested grebe offers a gift of water weed during a courtship display.*
*The double crest on the grebe's head is also raised during this display.*

**Penguin courtship** often involves the birds bowing to each other. Male adélie penguins perform an ecstatic display, stretching upward, inflating the neck, raising the head feathers, and beating the flippers.

**Male ostriches** display to females by waving their huge black-and-white wings, one after the other.

**Birds of prey** perform acrobatic "dances" in the air as part of their courtship display. They may swoop at each other and clasp talons.

**Courting mute swans** face each other, swaying their heads from side to side, or dipping their heads in the water and stretching their necks or bills in the air.

**To impress their partners**, blue-footed boobies show off their bright-blue feet, lifting and spreading their toes in a courtship dance.

53

# Defense

▲ *Terns nest together for safety and will dive-bomb intruders that enter their colonies.*

- **If a predator** comes near a killdeer's nest, the bird moves away, trailing a wing to look as though it is injured. The predator thinks it sees an easy victim and follows the bird. When the killdeer gets far enough away from the nest, it flies away.

- **Young jacanas** have special breathing holes at the tips of their bills. They use the holes like a snorkel to help them breathe when they dive underwater to escape danger.

- **Tawny owls** defend their nests and young fiercely, striking at intruders with their sharp talons, hissing, and spreading out their wings to make themselves look larger.

- **Flightless birds**, such as ostriches, emus, and kiwis, defend themselves with their sharp claws.

- **Ostriches** have a powerful kick, which may even be able to kill predators such as lions.

- **When birds** spot a predator, they give loud alarm calls and fly toward it, warning other birds and driving the predator away. This behavior is called mobbing.

- **Birds that nest** in large flocks, such as flamingos, warn each other of danger from every direction. Predators catch the slow, the sick, the old, and the unaware, making the flock stronger as a whole.

- **Penguins** use their hard, rigid flippers to fight off predators trying to attack their nesting colonies. They will also deliver a sharp bite.

- **Young burrowing owls** make a buzzing sound like a rattlesnake if they are threatened in their nesting burrow. This makes predators think twice about entering their burrow.

▼ A king penguin defends its egg from a brown skua. If a parent penguin leaves its egg or chick alone for even a few minutes, predators such as skuas quickly move in to attack.

55

# Bird songs and sounds

- **Birds make two main sorts of sounds**—simple calls, giving a warning or a threat, and the more complicated songs sung by some males at breeding time.

- **Birds' songs** have a definite dialect. The songs of a group of chaffinches in one area will sound slightly different from those of a group somewhere else.

- **A songbird** reared in captivity away from its family produces a weak version of its parents' song, but cannot perform the whole repertoire.

- **Gulls and parrots** do not sing, but they do make various calls to attract mates or warn off enemies.

- **A bird sings** by vibrating the thin muscles in its syrinx—a special organ in its throat.

- **A sedge warbler** may use at least 50 different sounds in its songs.

- **Male and female boubou shrikes** sing a duet together, performing alternate parts of the song.

- **Songbirds** may make as many as 20 calls; gulls make only about ten.

- **Birds make** other sounds too. During courtship flights, male wood pigeons make a loud clapping noise with their wings.

**DID YOU KNOW?**
A baby songbird starts to learn to sing about ten days after it hatches, and continues to learn for about 40 days.

◀ *Male nightingales sing to attract a mate and defend their territory. They sing more loudly in urban areas to make themselves heard above all the loud noise around them.*

# Nests

- **The bald eagle's nest** can be as large as 8 ft across and 11.5 ft deep—big enough for several people to hide inside!

- **The bee hummingbird's nest** is the smallest—only the size of a thimble.

- **The hammerkop**, a heronlike bird, makes a huge nest up to 6.5 ft high and weighing 110 lb. It uses anything from sticks to bits of bone and plastic to make its nest.

- **A cliff swallow's nest** is made up of about 1,200 tiny mud balls.

- **Nightjars** do not make a nest—they just lay their eggs on the ground.

▼ *The black-shouldered kite builds a large, untidy stick nest, about 3.3 ft wide, high in a tree. The male usually collects the nest material and the female builds the nest.*

▶ *The eggs of the ringed plover are laid in a shallow hollow, scraped in sand or shingle along the shoreline. The eggs are well camouflaged against the background since the nest gives them little protection.*

**Hummingbirds** and honeyeaters use spiders' webs to hold their nests together.

**The rufous-breasted castle builder** makes a nest shaped like a dumbbell with a tube linking both chambers. Only one of the chambers is used to rear the young.

**The turquoise-browed motmot** is a surprisingly efficient digger, excavating a 5-ft-long burrow in just five days.

**The European bee-eater** nests underground to keep cool. While the surface temperature may reach 122°F, the bee-eater's nest remains a pleasant 77°F.

# Unusual nests

- **The tailorbird** makes a cradlelike nest from two leaves, which it sews together with plant fibers or spiders' webs.

- **The female great Indian hornbill** incubates her eggs in a tree hole, the entrance of which is walled up with chewed bark and mud. The male passes her food through a slitlike opening in the wall.

- **Hornbills** keep their nests clean by pushing any food waste and droppings out through the slit opening.

- **The nest of a rufous hornero**, or ovenbird, is made of up to 2,500 lumps of mud and is about the size of a soccer ball.

- **Flamingos** nest on top of heaps of mud, which they make with their bills. Their mud nests protect their eggs and young from flooding, as well as the intense heat of the ground.

- **The horned coot** of the Andes builds a huge pile of stones under the water. It then builds its nest at the water's surface, on top of the artificial island of stones.

◀ *The rufous hornero's nest has walls about 1.2 in thick and a narrow entrance tunnel to protect the nesting chamber inside.*

**DID YOU KNOW?**
It takes 18 days or more for the rufous hornero to finish its oven-shaped mud nest.

Males weave
the nests

Narrow
entrance
tunnel

nale inside
oven nest

▲ *Weaverbirds loop, knot, and twist grass stems together with their beaks to make complex woven nests. Narrow entrance tunnels face downward, making it difficult for predators to get inside.*

🦃 **The pear-shaped, hanging nest** of the penduline tit is very strong and so densely woven that predators cannot tear it apart. These soft nests are used as purses or slippers in some parts of the world.

🦃 **Australian brush turkeys** build large mounds of leaves and soil up to 5 ft high and 13 ft across. The eggs develop in the warmth of these giant compost piles.

🦃 **Male brush turkeys** check the temperature of nest mounds with their bills and regulate the temperature by adding or removing nest material.

# Nesting in colonies

- **About one in eight** bird species worldwide nest in colonies (large groups). Nesting colonies are common among seabirds and waterbirds, such as herons and storks.

- **Birds in a colony** start building their nests, lay their eggs, raise their young, and roost (sleep) at the same time.

- **There is safety in numbers**, and birds in a colony also help each other to locate food sources. The disadvantages of colonial living include competition for space, food, and mates, as well as the danger of diseases spreading quickly.

- **The sociable weaver** nests in groups of up to 300 birds. Each huge nest is made of sticks and grass, normally in a large acacia tree. A nest may measure 13 ft deep and weigh up to 220 lb, and each pair of birds has its own hole in the nest.

- **Great white pelican breeding colonies** may number as many as 30,000 pairs of birds.

- **Flamingos** live in flocks that are hundreds of thousands of birds strong in the breeding season.

- **Many seabirds** nest in colonies on steep cliffs, where it is difficult for predators to reach their eggs and young. Different species share out the available nesting sites by nesting at different levels.

- **Penguins build their nests** close together, pecking distance apart, and defend the small area around their nests fiercely. As rival penguins fight each other, nests and chicks may be trampled. In some cases, penguins may even kill each other.

- **Cormorants** nest in such large colonies that huge deposits of their droppings, known as guano, build up. People sometimes collect this guano to use as fertilizer.

- **One of the largest** gannet nesting colonies in the world is at Bass Rock, 30 mi from Edinburgh at the mouth of the Firth of Forth in Scotland, U.K. Gannets pair for life and use the same nest site year after year.

▼ *Most penguins nest in vast colonies. This is partly because there is little land free of ice in areas of the Antarctic where they nest.*

# Eggs

- **All bird species** lay eggs.

- **The biggest egg** is the ostrich egg. At 3.3 lb, it is 30 times heavier than an average hen's egg.

- **Incubation is the process** of keeping eggs warm while they develop. It can take between ten and 80 days.

- **The yolk** in an egg provides nourishment for the embryo (developing young). The white provides food and moisture and protects the yolk.

▼ A bird's egg, though seemingly simple, contains everything that the growing embryo inside needs to survive.

First tiny hole

Egg cracks

Chick appears

▶ When a chick is ready to hatch, it makes a tiny hole in the shell with its "egg tooth" —a process called "pipping"— and then struggles out.

Chick breaks free of egg

🪶 **Egg yolks** are not always yellow. The common tern's yolk is deep red and the gentoo penguin's is a pinky red.

🪶 **Gannets stand on their eggs** to keep them warm!

🪶 **The shell of an egg** contains tiny pores. This means that oxygen can pass through the shell to the baby bird inside and carbon dioxide can pass out.

🪶 **Eggshells vary in thickness** from 0.2 mm in the night heron's egg, to 0.75 mm in the common murre's.

🪶 **Not all eggs are oval**—those of owls and toucans are round, and auks lay pear-shaped eggs.

# Helpless young

▲ *The bright red color inside the mouths of these chicks stimulates their parents to feed them.*

🐦 **Many baby birds** are blind, naked (without feathers), and helpless when they hatch. They have to be cared for by their parents.

🐦 **A young golden eagle** grows its adult feathers after 50 days and learns to fly after 70, but stays with its parents for another month while learning to hunt.

🐦 **A young pelican** feeds by putting its head deep into its parent's large beak and gobbling up any fish it finds.

🐦 **In three weeks**, a newly hatched cuckoo becomes 50 times heavier.

🐦 **Helpless baby birds** are called "altricial young." The word altricial comes from the Latin word *alere*, meaning "to rear or nourish."

- **Birds such as herons**, hawks, woodpeckers, crows, cardinals, owls, magpies, lorikeets, wrens, pigeons, and sparrows all have altricial young.

- **Altricial birds** lay smaller eggs and build strong nests to protect them, usually in trees, bushes, or shrubs. One or both of the parents incubates (sits on) the eggs to keep them warm.

- **Altricial young**, or nestlings, grow quickly, develop feathers, and usually leave the nest within two to four weeks. Most nestlings grow to the same size as their parents in this short space of time.

- **When they fledge** (leave the nest), altricial young are called fledglings.

- **Parent birds** care for fledglings for a short time after they leave the nest, until they are completely independent. New fledglings often follow their parents around and beg for food.

▲ Hoopoes nest inside holes in trees or walls. Both parents feed the young, which stay in the nest hole for about four weeks.

67

# Independent young

- **Precocial baby birds** are much more developed than altricial baby birds when they hatch out of their eggs.

- **Birds with precocial chicks** include emus, ducks, lapwings, gulls, geese, swans, brush turkeys, terns, and many wading shorebirds.

- **Precocial young** are covered with down feathers, have their eyes open, and can run around or swim soon after hatching.

- **Some precocial chicks** can feed themselves soon after hatching, while others, such as gulls and terns, depend on their parents for food.

- **To obtain food** from its parent, a young herring gull has to peck at a red spot on the parent's beak. The adult gull then regurgitates food for the chick to eat.

- **With their fluffy feathers**, precocial chicks can usually keep themselves warm without help from their parents.

◀ Ducklings cannot produce the oil that waterproofs their feathers until they are between three and four weeks old. In the wild, a mother duck oils her duckling's feathers until they can do this for themselves.

▶ Swans are attentive parents—the female usually incubates the eggs but the male is equally involved in raising the young. Chicks are tended for about five months after they hatch.

- **A swan** carries its young on its back to keep them safe.

- **Precocial chicks** usually hatch out in relatively simple nests on the ground and stay with their parents until they can look after themselves. They grow much more slowly than altricial birds and it takes them a long time, often two months or more, before they are able to fly.

- **Parents of precocial chicks** spend a lot of time watching out for predators, since their small, flightless chicks are vulnerable to attack until they grow their flight feathers.

**DID YOU KNOW?**
Even in a colony of thousands of birds, baby terns can recognize the call of their own parents.

69

# Why birds migrate

- **Migration** is the journey made by many animals twice a year between a summer breeding area, where food is plentiful, and a wintering area with a good climate.

- **Many migrating birds** have to build up fat stores to allow them to fly nonstop for days without food.

- **Some small birds** double their weight before migrating to provide them with enough energy stores for traveling long distances.

- **Most birds** that migrate long distances fly at night, when they are safer from predators.

- **Nearly half** of all the world's birds migrate.

▼ Geese migrate in huge flocks, but pairs stay together within the flock.

▶ Birds are sensitive to the position of the Earth's magnetic field, which helps them to navigate on migration journeys.

- **Birds find their way** by observing landmarks, the patterns of stars, and the position of the setting Sun. They also use their sense of smell and monitor Earth's magnetic field.

- **Some birds** migrate short distances. The Himalayan monal pheasant migrates up and down the mountains with the seasons, moving down to the warmer lower slopes in winter.

- **In the Northern Hemisphere**, birds tend to move south to warmer places in winter, while in the Southern Hemisphere, they fly north.

- **Many birds** migrate to the Arctic to nest during the brief summer months when there is plenty of food available there.

- **Before migration was studied**, some people thought swallows simply spent the winter asleep in mud.

# Migration journeys

- **A migrating bird** can fly across the Sahara desert in 50–60 hours without stopping to "refuel."

- **The snow goose** migrates nearly 3,000 mi south from Arctic Canada at an altitude of 29,500 ft.

- **Even flightless birds migrate**. Emus make journeys of 300 mi or more on foot and penguins migrate in water.

- **Every year** at least five billion birds migrate from North America to Central and South America.

- **The Arctic tern** spends the northern summer in the Arctic and migrates to the Antarctic for the southern summer, enjoying 24 hours of daylight in both places.

▼ A flock of migrating Canada geese follow in the slipstream of their leader to save energy.

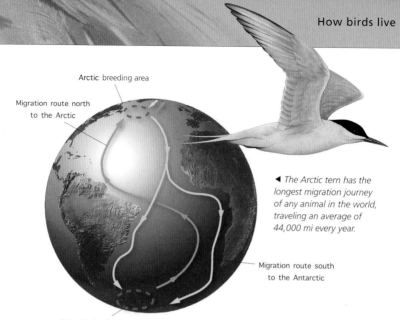

Arctic breeding area

Migration route north to the Arctic

◄ *The Arctic tern has the longest migration journey of any animal in the world, traveling an average of 44,000 mi every year.*

Migration route south to the Antarctic

Antarctic feeding area

🦜 **Although only 4 in long**, the little storm petrel may migrate 24,800 mi a year between the two poles.

🦜 **Flying in a V-shaped formation** helps birds to save energy on a long journey.

🦜 **Larger migrating birds,** such as cranes or storks, usually fly by day. They save energy by gliding on warm currents of air (thermals), which rise off the land.

🦜 **Most migrating birds** fly below 300 ft, although bar-headed geese cross the Himalayas at heights of 26,000 ft, white storks migrate at heights of 21,000 ft, and fieldfares may reach heights of 10,800 ft.

🦜 **The American golden plover** has the longest migration journey of all land birds. It breeds in northern Canada and flies south to the grasslands of Argentina for the winter.

73

# The Arctic

- **The willow ptarmigan** lives on the Arctic tundra. In winter, it has white feathers that help to keep it hidden in the snow, but in summer it grows darker feathers again.

- **The ivory gull** of Arctic coasts and islands is the only pure white gull.

- **Snowy owls** are among the fiercest Arctic birds. They soar over the tundra preying on other birds and small mammals, such as lemmings.

- **The laysan albatross** breeds on central Pacific islands, but spends most of the year flying over the Arctic hunting for schools of fish to eat.

▲ The willow ptarmigan, shown here in the process of changing into its white winter coat, feeds mainly on the leaves and shoots of plants, such as dwarf willows, but also eats berries, seeds, and insects.

- **Tufted puffins** nest only on cliffs and islands in the Arctic North Pacific. One colony contained as many as one million nests.

- **The auks** of the Arctic look similar to the penguins of the Antarctic because they have similar lifestyles. Unlike penguins, auks can fly, as well as using their wings to swim underwater as they chase prey.

- **Little auks** are resident in the Arctic all year round. They have dense feathers and a thick layer of fat under their skin to keep them warm.

**DID YOU KNOW?**

Over 100 million little auks, or dovekies, breed along Arctic coasts each summer.

- **Snow buntings** may burrow in the snow to escape the intense cold of the Arctic.

- **Ravens** are one of the few birds able to survive the cold Arctic climate all year round. Their black feathers help them to absorb heat.

- **Tundra swans** nest on the treeless land around the Arctic, which is called the tundra. They migrate south for the winter.

▶ The snowy owl's white feathers help to camouflage it in its Arctic home.

# The Antarctic

- **Giant petrels** are about the size of vultures, with a wingspan of nearly 6.5 ft. They will eat almost anything, including dead seals and whales.

- **Sheathbills** are the only land birds that live all year round in the Antarctic. They are named after the horny sheath that protects their nostrils.

- **Blue-eyed cormorants** nest in noisy, smelly colonies near the sea. Their nests are made of heaps of seaweed, lichens, mosses, and feathers, glued together with bird droppings.

▲ The sheathbill is an aggressive scavenger. It lives and breeds solely in Antarctica and its immediate regions, such as the Falkland Islands and the most southerly areas of South America.

- **Only two species** of penguin, the emperor and the Adélie, breed on the continent of Antarctica, but gentoo, macaroni, chinstrap, rockhopper, and king penguins all breed within Antarctic waters.

- **Penguins** huddle together to keep warm in the icy cold Antarctic. A tightly packed group of penguins can reduce heat loss by up to 50 percent.

- **Adélie penguins** breed on coasts and islands around the Antarctic in huge colonies that return to the same site year after year.

- **The emperor penguin** breeds in colder temperatures than any other bird. It can survive temperatures of -40°F as it incubates its egg.

- **Skuas** are large, aggressive birds that often steal the eggs and chicks of other birds. They have powerful bills to stab and kill their prey.

- **The great skua** is the biggest flying bird in Antarctica, weighing up to 11 lb and measuring 26 in long.

- **Most birds leave Antarctica in winter**, but the southern black-backed gull stays all year round. It feeds on fish and birds' eggs as well as some carrion.

▼ *Adélie penguins may have to travel up to 62 mi from the sea to reach their breeding colonies in the Antarctic. More than two million pairs of these penguins nest in the Antarctic each year.*

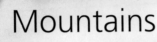

# Mountains

- **The alpine accentor** breeds high in the mountains, and has been seen nesting at 26,250 ft in the Himalayas.

- **The wallcreeper** is an expert climber and can clamber up steep cliffs and walls in its search for insect prey. It lives high in mountains such as the Alps and Himalayas.

- **Torrent ducks** live by fast-flowing streams in South America's Andes mountains. When new ducklings hatch, they leap straight into the swirling waters.

- **The Himalayan snowcock** (partridge family) lives on the lower slopes of the Himalayas, where its gray-and-white feathers hide it among rocks and snow.

◀ Golden eagles use rising columns of hot air (thermals) to soar up into the sky, from where they can spot prey such as rabbits, hares, and grouse on the ground below. They catch and kill prey in their huge, bone-crushing talons.

- **The Himalayan monal pheasant** spends some of the year above the tree line, where it has to dig in the snow with its beak to find insects and other food.

- **The lammergeier**, or bearded vulture, has a long, thin tongue shaped like a garden trowel, which helps it to scoop the nutritious marrow from inside bones.

- **The hill mynah** lives in the treetops on the lower slopes of the Himalayan mountains. It feeds mainly on fruits and nectar.

- **The mountain chickadee** nests in forests in the Rocky Mountains in spring and summer, but moves down to warmer valleys in the cold winter months. There it feeds in mixed flocks with other small birds.

- **The golden eagle** is one of the most common birds in all the world's mountain ranges. It flies well in the strong winds and has keen eyesight to spot prey, such as mountain hares, as it soars above the steep slopes.

- **Verreaux's eagle** hunts in the mountains and hills of Africa and the Middle East, preying on small mammals such as hyraxes.

▶ *The nimble wallcreeper clings to rock faces with its sharp claws, probing for insects with its long, slender bill.*

# Conifer forests

◄ *The great gray owl can hear its prey moving in tunnels beneath the snow in winter and swoops down to grab a meal.*

■ **The black-backed three-toed woodpecker** lives in the conifer forests of North America. It moves its bill from side to side to remove loose bark from trees and reach the beetle grubs underneath.

■ **The capercaillie** has comblike fringes on its toes to help it walk on snow without sinking in.

■ **During its courtship display**, the male capercaillie fans out its tail, puffs out its throat feathers, points its bill in the air, and makes extraordinary popping and gurgling sounds.

■ **Clark's nutcracker** hides 4,000 or more conifer tree seeds in the fall. It can remember where it stored these seeds for up to nine months, helping it to survive the winter.

■ **The great gray owl** uses its very keen hearing to detect the rustling sounds made by small mammals on the forest floor.

- **Male spruce grouse** display to females by fluttering or whirring their wings, either when perched on a log or flying through the air.

- **The acrobatic coal tit** is able to survive the cold winters in coniferous forests because it feeds on insects living beneath tree bark. It nests in tree holes, building a cup-shaped nest from moss, hair, and feathers.

- **Siskins** depend on the seeds of pine and spruce trees for food in spring and early summer. They build their nests near the end of conifer tree branches at least 16 ft above the ground.

- **The goshawk** lays its eggs on a large platform of sticks, lined with leaves or pine needles. The female incubates the eggs for about five months until they hatch.

- **The goldcrest** spends most of its time searching for food high in the tops of conifer trees. It is the smallest European bird.

▼ *Pine forests are a favorite habitat of the crested tit, which moves along tree trunks like a treecreeper, picking insects from the bark with its pointed bill.*

# Deciduous woodlands

- **Blue jays** have a loud, screeching, harsh call, which they often use as an alarm to warn of a predator, such as a hawk or an owl.

- **Long-tailed tits** build elaborate nests of moss, cobwebs, and hair, lined with thousands of feathers to keep their young warm.

- **A woodcock's** mottled brown plumage gives it perfect camouflage among the fallen leaves on the woodland floor.

- **Bees and wasps**, their larvae, and even their nests are the main food of honey buzzards, which remove the stings from adult insects before eating them.

- **Wrynecks** are named after their strange habit of twisting and contorting their necks when they are startled or threatened. These birds also twist their necks during courtship.

- **Up to half** of the birds that nest in woodlands do so in holes in dead or decaying trees. They usually build only a small, simple nest inside a tree hole.

- **In spring**, many birds, such as chiffchaffs, travel from their winter feeding grounds in Africa to woodlands in Europe, where they nest and raise their young.

- **A sparrowhawk** has short, wide, rounded wings to help it fly through small spaces in woodlands as it chases small birds, such as blue tits. The long, flexible tail is like a rudder and helps the sparrowhawk to change direction quickly.

▶ A sparrowhawk uses its sharp, hooked bill to pluck the feathers from a siskin before it starts to feed.

# American rain forests

- **With its abundance** of flowers, leaves, fruits, and insects, a rain forest is the ideal home for many different kinds of birds.

- **One fifth** of all bird species live in the Amazon rain forest.

- **Toucans** live in noisy groups and often play games. They may wrestle with their huge bills and throw fruit to each other in a game of "treetop catch."

- **Young hoatzins** may leap into the water beneath their riverside nests in order to escape danger.

- **Flocks of brightly colored macaws** sometimes feed on soil because it is rich in minerals and keeps them healthy.

- **Quetzals** feed on avocado trees and help to spread the trees' seeds through the forest in their droppings. The trees and the birds help each other to survive.

- **The king vulture** of South America is the only vulture to live in rain forests. As well as feeding on carrion, it also kills mammals and reptiles.

◀ The tropical rain forest has more types of bird than anywhere else. Many of the birds in the canopy are amazingly colorful. Gamebirds and little insect eaters patrol the forest floor.

**The sunbittern** lives along river banks in the rain forests of South America, feeding on frogs, insects, and other creatures.

**The muscovy duck** is now familiar in farmyards and parks in many parts of the world. However, it originally came from the rain forests of Central and South America.

**The spectacled eagle owl** of South America has rings of white feathers around its eyes. Its call resembles the hammering sound made by woodpeckers.

| 1 Junglefowl | 4 Harpy eagle |
| --- | --- |
| 2 Scarlet macaw | 5 Hoatzin |
| 3 Quetzal | 6 Congo peafowl |

# African and Asian rain forests

- **The crowned eagle** lives in African rain forests, where it feeds on monkeys and other mammals, such as mongooses and rats.

- **Large, flightless cassowaries** live in the rain forests of New Guinea, where people hunt them to eat.

- **The rare Cassin's hawk eagle** lives in African rain forests, and hunts squirrels and other birds.

- **The lesser green broadbill** feeds in flocks, searching for fruit, buds, and insects. It makes whistling and bubbling noises as it feeds, sounding rather like a frog.

◄ The enormous Philippine eagle swoops down to catch a flying squirrel.

▶ *A male Raggiana bird of paradise shows off its long, colorful feathers in a courtship display that can last for hours.*

**The male argus pheasant** clears a patch of forest floor in the breeding season so it can strut up and down, calling loudly to attract females.

**The hornbills of Africa** and the toucans of South America look similar because they live, feed, and survive in a similar way. This is called convergent evolution.

**The Asian leafbird** helps to spread the pollen of the forest trees as it feeds on nectar. It also spreads the seeds of plants in the mistletoe family by eating the berries and depositing the seeds in its droppings.

**Male Raggiana birds of paradise** display together in the rain forests of New Guinea, shrieking loudly to attract the attention of females.

**Bowerbirds** sometimes decorate their bowers with old bottle tops and other litter thrown away by people.

# American grasslands

▲ *During his courtship display, the male greater prairie chicken inflates the orange air sacs on his neck and makes a hollow booming call.*

**A variety** of seed and insect-eating birds live in grasslands. Some of them follow herds of grazing animals and catch the insects disturbed by their feet.

**One of the biggest creatures** on the South American pampas is the rhea, which feeds mainly on grass.

**The long legs** of rheas help them to see over the tall grasses of the South American pampas and watch for predators. They are flightless birds so cannot fly to escape danger.

**Common caracaras** are birds of prey that are related to falcons. They have a varied diet and often join vultures to feed on a carcass.

DID YOU KNOW?
The western meadowlark makes a ground nest of grass and pine needles in prairie grasslands.

- **The mottled patterns** on the crested tinamou's feathers help to camouflage it from predators on the open grasslands of South America. It is not good at flying, but can run fast for short distances.

- **The burrowing owl** nests in burrows in the ground, either digging its own with its strong claws, or taking over the burrows of other animals, such as prairie dogs.

- **The grasslands of South America** are home to the red-legged seriema, a long-legged, fast-running bird that eats virtually anything it can find, including snakes.

- **The crested oropendola** is a grassland bird of South America. It hunts insects and other small creatures.

- **North America's largest owl**, the great horned owl, includes other grassland birds, such as quail, in its diet.

▶ Unlike most owls, burrowing owls are often active during the day. They run over the grasslands on their long legs, catching insects and small reptiles in their talons.

# African grasslands

- **The yellow-billed oxpecker** of the African grasslands sits on buffaloes' backs, pulling ticks from their skin.

- **Flocks of one million or more red-billed quelea** are seen moving like vast clouds over southern Africa.

- **Unlike most hornbills,** the southern ground hornbill of southern Africa spends most of its time on the ground.

- **Cattle egrets** accompany large grassland mammals, feeding on the insects that live on or around them.

- **Many honeyguides** lay their eggs in the nests of other birds, such as woodpeckers. When they hatch, the young honeyguides kill the chicks of the host bird.

▼ *Marabou storks are the only storks to eat carrion (dead animals). They often gather with vultures at animal carcasses, where the vultures give way to these aggressive storks, letting them eat first.*

92

- **Vultures** feed on other grassland animals when they die. Their bare heads and necks allow them to feed inside animal carcasses without getting their feathers dirty.

- **After a meal**, vultures always clean their feathers to keep them in good condition for flying.

- **Carmine bee-eaters** live in colonies numbering hundreds of birds. They dig burrows in the soil, often in sandy banks, and lay their eggs at the end of the burrows.

▲ The oxpecker is so-called because it often pecks at wounds in the skin of grassland mammals while pulling ticks from their skin.

- **Female paradise whydahs** lay their eggs in the nests of melba finches. When they hatch out, the young whydahs copy the calls and behavior of the young finches so their foster parents will feed them.

▶ The red-billed quelea is a common sight in grassland areas across the southern African continent.

93

# American deserts

- **The verdin** lives in the deserts of Mexico and the southwest of the U.S., where it makes its nest on cactus plants. The cactus spines protect the verdin and its eggs from predators.

- **With few trees and bushes to sit in,** desert birds spend most of their lives on the ground.

- **The mourning dove** is a desert bird of the southwestern U.S. A fast flier, it often travels great distances to find food and water.

- **Turkey vultures** soar over the American deserts searching for carrion to eat.

- **Owls, poorwills, and nightjars** cool down in the desert heat by opening their mouths wide and fluttering their throats.

- **Water is precious** in the desert. The roadrunner, a member of the cuckoo family, reabsorbs water from its faeces before excretion.

- **The greater roadrunner** sprints at up to 15 mph on its long, powerful legs. It flutters its short stubby wings to provide extra speed and uses its long tail as a brake, or to help it change direction.

▼ The greater roadrunner lives in the western U.S., where it preys on small snakes as well as insects and mice.

Elf owl

Hummingbirds

Gila
woodpecker

▲ *Elf owls shelter from the heat of the day in giant cacti, inside holes that are
dug out by other birds, such as the gila woodpecker.*

- **The gila woodpecker** digs out a nesting hole in the stem of a
  desert cactus. It is much cooler inside the cactus and the spines
  help to protect its young from predators.

- **The smallest owl** in the world, the elf owl, comes out at night to
  escape the heat of the day.

- **The elf owl** feeds mainly on insects, but will also eat desert
  scorpions, taking out the sting before eating its meal.

95

# Other deserts

- **Insects are a favorite food** of many desert birds, but some catch small mammals and others eat seeds.

- **Most desert birds** are active at dawn and toward sunset, resting in shade for much of the day.

**DID YOU KNOW?**

Budgerigars roam the deserts of the Australian outback in flocks of thousands. They fly hundreds of miles in search of water.

▼ *Spinifex pigeons live in the harsh deserts of Australia. For their survival, they depend on the waterholes that fill with water in the wet season.*

🪶 **Sooty falcon chicks** hatch out in late summer, when there are many small birds migrating across the Sahara desert in northern Africa. This provides a good food supply for the parent falcons to feed to their chicks.

🪶 **The little cinnamon quail-thrush** of Australia hides in a burrow during the day to escape the hot sun, and comes out in the evening to find seeds and insects to eat.

🪶 **The sandgrouse** travels up to 30 mi a day to fetch water for its young chicks in the nest.

🪶 **The emus of Australia** are related to the ostriches of Africa, but emus have three toes on each foot, while ostriches have only two toes on each foot.

🪶 **Emus store fat in their bodies** when food is plentiful. This helps them to survive times when food is scarce.

🪶 **Emu chicks** hatch out of emerald-green eggs and have striped feathers for camouflage. They can walk within a few hours of hatching and run within days.

▶ *A male sandgrouse soaks its belly feathers at a desert waterhole, then flies back to its nest so the chicks can drink from its plumage.*

# Rivers, lakes, and swamps

- **The five species of dipper** live in Europe, Asia, and parts of North and South America.

- **The dome-shaped nests** of dippers usually have an entrance over running water.

- **The 31 species of ibis and spoonbill** live in North and South America, southern Europe, Asia, Africa, and Australia, often in wetlands.

- **The marsh harrier** flies close to the ground searching for mice, rats, frogs, rabbits, and even fish. When it spots prey, it swoops down, seizes the victim in its sharp talons, and tears it apart with its beak.

- **The largest of the heron family** is the goliath heron of Africa and Southwest Asia—it measures 5 ft in length.

▼ The dipper is the only type of songbird to live in and around water—it can swim underwater and even walk along stream beds as it searches for insect prey.

▲ *Roseate spoonbills catch food, such as fish, by sweeping their sensitive bills from side to side through shallow water.*

- **The snail kite's hook-tipped beak** is perfectly shaped for extracting the soft flesh of snails from their shells.

- **The jagged edges** of an anhinga's bill help it to keep a firm grip on slippery fish until it can flip them up into the air and swallow them whole.

- **The shoveler duck** has a wide, shovel-shaped bill with combs inside for filtering tiny floating animals and plants from the water.

- **The whale-headed stork** has a huge, shoe-shaped bill, which helps it to catch its favorite food—lungfish. In hot weather, parent whale-headed storks sometimes collect water in their bills and pour it over their chicks to keep them cool.

# Seabirds

◄ The red-billed tropicbird's narrow tail streamers are almost the same length as its body. They may help to stabilize the bird in flight and are also used during the courtship display.

🦃 **The white-tailed tropicbird** is noted for its amazing tail streamers, which can measure up to 16 in long.

🦃 **The three species of tropicbird** are all experts in the air and can dive into the sea to find prey, but cannot walk on land. With their legs set far back on their bodies, they are only able to drag themselves along.

🦃 **An albatross** may fly 10 million mi in a lifetime, soaring over the ocean waves on its long, powerful wings.

🦃 **Manx shearwaters** nest in colonies, usually in burrows on remote islands. They come ashore at night to tend to their chicks, in order to avoid attacks from great black-backed gulls.

🦃 **Diving petrels** have small wings, which they use to "fly" underwater to catch food.

**In the 19th century**, the droppings (guano) in seabird colonies off the coast of Peru reached depths of 150 ft. Today, people have harvested most of the guano and it is only about one foot deep.

**DID YOU KNOW?**

Fulmars defend themselves by squirting predators with a horrible smelly oil, produced from their stomachs. Even a young fulmar chick can defend itself in this way.

**Shags can be distinguished** from cormorants by the lack of a white patch on their face.

**Great skuas** dive-bomb intruders to their nest site, kicking them with their webbed feet and pecking them with their powerful bill.

**The courtship flight** of the sandwich tern includes a "fish flight," which involves the male offering the female a fish in midair.

▼ Guillemots spend a lot of time far out at sea, coming to land only to rest or breed on coastal cliffs.

101

# Coastal birds

- **Ringed plovers** nest on beaches in a hollow scraped in the sand or shingle. Their fluffy chicks are well camouflaged and can run about almost as soon as they hatch.

- **The purple sandpiper** feeds near the edge of the sea, picking up shellfish, worms, and insects at a rapid rate.

- **If danger threatens** its nest, a sanderling may pretend to have an injured wing and flutters away to draw the predator away from its eggs or chicks.

- **Huge flocks** of dunlin fly in closely knit flocks along the shore at high tide, looking from a distance like billowing clouds of smoke.

- **Inca terns** roost in large flocks on sandy beaches. They are graceful fliers, often hovering over the water before dipping down to snatch a fish.

- **Skimmers** have unusual vertical pupils, which can be closed to slits in bright sunshine or opened wide in poor light.

- **Guillemot chicks** leave their nest sites on coastal cliffs at around three weeks old. This means their parents can lead them to a food supply instead of bringing food long distances back to the nest.

- **The marbled murrelet** is named after the pale edges to its feathers, which give it a mottled appearance, especially in the breeding season.

- **Puffins** use their beaks to dig nesting burrows on grassy cliff tops. The burrows can be several feet long.

- **The swallow-tailed gull** has large, forward-facing eyes, which help it to find food at night.

1 Great black-backed gull

2 Lesser black-backed gull

3 Herring gull

4 Rock dove

5 Chough

6 Puffin

7 Guillemot

8 Razorbill

9 Rock pipit

10 Fulmar

11 Kittiwake

12 Black guillemot

▶ Many seabirds nest in colonies on steep cliffs, where it is difficult for predators to reach their eggs and young. Different species share out the available nesting sites by nesting at different levels.

103

# Island birds

- **About 17 percent** of the world's bird species live only on islands.

- **The world's smallest flightless bird**, the Inaccessible Island rail, weighs only 1.2 oz—about the same as a small tomato. It lives on Inaccessible Island in the South Atlantic Ocean.

- **Gough Island** in the South Atlantic Ocean provides a sheltered site for about two million nesting seabirds, including almost the entire population of the Tristan albatross and the Atlantic petrel.

- **The almost flightless** Gough Island moorhen and the critically endangered Gough bunting are also found on Gough Island.

- **The Galápagos penguin** is able to survive on islands so near the Equator because of the cold waters of the Humboldt Current, which flow past the Galápagos Islands.

- **The 13 species** of Galápagos finches probably evolved from a common ancestor. Each species has a different shaped bill to eat a different sort of food, such as insects or seeds.

▶ Galápagos penguins usually feed at sea during the day and come ashore at night, when it is cooler. They hold out their flippers to encourage the wind to blow heat away from their body and cool them down.

▲ *The Galápagos woodpecker finch uses a twig to prise insect grubs out of tree bark. It is one of the few birds to make and use a tool, which is a sign of intelligence.*

**A group of birds** called the vanga shrikes live only on the island of Madagascar, off the coast of Africa.

**The coral-billed nuthatch vanga** lives in the rain forests of eastern Madagascar. It clings to tree trunks with its sharp claws and uses its bill to probe under the bark for insect grubs.

**Mikado pheasants** live only on the island of Taiwan. Both males and females have long tails.

**The Japanese white-eye** lives on the island of Honshu. In summer, this bird soaks up nectar from flowers with a brush-tipped tongue.

# Urban birds

- **In some European cities**, white storks nest on chimneys and are supposed to bring good fortune to the people who live there.

- **Wild pigeons** roost and nest on cliffs and city pigeons now make their homes on the artificial cliffs of our cities.

- **Swallows, swifts, and house martins** were originally cave or cliff dwellers, but now nest on or in buildings.

- **Barn owls** have even nested in the belfry of the cathedral of Notre Dame in Paris!

- **Egyptian vultures** and marabou storks search for food scraps among the town and city rubbish dumps of Africa.

- **Rainbow lorikeets** live in city suburbs in Australia and often visit bird tables. In parts of Queensland, huge flocks of rainbow and scaly-breasted lorikeets are fed as a tourist display.

- **Urban birds** nest in unusual places, from old vacuum cleaners and empty paint pots to street lights and mailboxes. Their nesting materials include string and telephone wire.

- **Many Canada geese** remain in city parks all year round, instead of migrating to warmer places for the winter.

- **Falcons have adapted well** to city life—kestrels hover above garbage cans to watch for mice, and peregrines dive down between New York skyscrapers.

- **Some crows in Japan** have learned to use cars to crack nuts. They drop the nuts in front of cars waiting at traffic lights, wait for the cars to drive over the nuts, then collect them once the lights turn red again!

▼ The flocks of pigeons on city streets are mainly descended from domesticated birds reared as a source of food. Some of these birds escaped into the wild and started to live an urban lifestyle.

DID YOU KNOW?

House sparrows have been recorded nesting down a coal mine in the U.K. They were fed by the miners over 650 ft below the ground.

# Perching birds

# What is a perching bird?

🐦 **Perching birds**, or passerines, belong to the order Passeriformes, which contains more than 5,700 bird species. Passeriformes means "sparrow-shaped."

🐦 **Almost 60 percent** of the bird species in the world today are passerines.

🐦 **Passerines** are probably the most advanced, intelligent, and well adapted birds.

🐦 **Perching birds** are usually small land birds that eat mainly seeds, fruit, nectar, and insects.

🐦 **The largest perching birds** are the ravens and Australian lyrebirds. The smallest are the bushtits and pygmy tits.

🐦 **All perching birds** share the same type of foot, which is adapted to grip a perch tightly. If a bird begins to fall off its perch, the muscles and tendons in the legs automatically tighten their grip. This allows a perching bird to sleep without falling off its perch.

🐦 **Many perching birds** are songbirds and have complex muscles to control the syrinx—a sound-producing organ in the throat.

🐦 **Most perching birds** lay colored eggs, whereas the eggs of other birds are usually white.

🐦 **The chicks** of perching birds do not have feathers when they hatch out. They are blind and helpless, so need a lot of parental care.

🐦 **Many baby perching birds** gape widely to beg for food from their parents while they are in the nest.

▶ *Eurasian jays are the most colorful members of the crow family. These shy woodlands birds have a loud, screeching call.*

# Crows, rooks, and ravens

- **Members of the crow family** live on all continents of the world, except Antarctica. There are about 117 species, including jackdaws, rooks, ravens, nutcrackers, choughs, and jays, as well as common crows.

- **Bold and aggressive**, a typical crow is a big bird with a strong body, strong legs, and a powerful beak that can deal with nuts, seeds, and even small prey.

- **Crows** are thought to be among the most intelligent of all birds. Studies on ravens have shown that they are able to count up to five or six.

- **A species of crow** that lives on the Pacific island of New Caledonia uses tools, such as hooked twigs and sharp-ended stems, to extract grubs from the crowns of palm trees.

- **At 26 in long**, the raven is the largest member of the crow family, with a wingspan of nearly 5 ft.

- **In spring**, jackdaws collect soft fibers for their nests and they may even pluck wool from sheeps' backs.

- **Famous for their acrobatic skills** in the air, choughs (pronounced "chuffs") swoop and soar on their broad, rounded wings, with their wingtips spread out like fingers. Courting choughs take part in a display flight before nesting.

- **Choughs are mainly** mountain birds. They live at altitudes of nearly 29,500 ft in the Himalayas.

🦅 **Breeding pairs** of Australian white-winged choughs use a team of up to eight other choughs to help them find food for their young.

🦅 **Great spotted cuckoos** often lay their eggs in the nests of pied crows, causing some of the pied crow chicks to starve.

▶ The secret of the crow's success is its adaptability. Crows eat a wide range of foods and are intelligent enough to learn how to make use of new food sources. Shown here are:
1 raven, 2 rook,
3 hooded crow,
4 chough,
5 jackdaw.

113

# Jays, magpies, and nutcrackers

- **North American blue jays** are noisy, bold birds, which often visit parks and gardens. They migrate in spring and the fall.

- **The gray jay**, or Canada jay, stores food for the winter in conifer trees, rather than on the ground as other jays do. This is because the forest floor where it lives is covered with snow in winter.

- **The gray jay** glues spruce seeds and other food to the leaves of conifer trees with its own saliva, so it has extra-large salivary glands.

- **Scrub jays** live in groups of up to 12 birds. Only one pair of birds in the group breeds, while the "helpers" stand guard at the nest site or gather food.

Eurasian black-billed magpie

Azure-winged magpie

▶ Magpies and jays are adaptable eaters and take a very wide range of food.

American blue jay

Eurasian jay

- **Jays may chase each other** through the trees as part of their courtship display. The male birds raise their crests and body feathers to impress the females.

- **When food is plentiful**, nutcrackers hide nuts and pine seeds in holes in the ground, and are able to find them again months later.

- **Clark's nutcracker** may fly 12.5 mi to gather food for its winter store, carrying up to 80 seeds in a pouch beneath its tongue.

▲ Clark's nutcracker feeds mainly on the seeds of conifer trees, such as the Ponderosa pine. It uses its powerful bill to prise the seeds from cones.

- **The seeds** buried by jays and nutcrackers as winter food stores help trees to spread, since the birds do not recover all of their seeds. Some of the seeds sprout into new trees.

- **The Asian green magpie** often feeds in mixed flocks with drongos and laughing thrushes. It eats insects, snakes, lizards, frogs, and young birds, as well as scavenging for carrion.

- **Azure-winged magpies** usually feed in small groups, roost together, and nest in loose colonies.

**DID YOU KNOW?**

Magpies steal the eggs and young of other birds, as well as bright, shiny objects, such as jewelry, which they hide in their nests.

115

# Swallows and martins

🔸 **There are about 80 species** of swallows and martins found all over the world. Most migrate between breeding grounds and wintering areas.

🔸 **In most swallow species**, males and females are alike, but in the rare blue swallow, the female has a short tail, while the male's is long and forked.

🔸 **Swallows** catch their insect food in the air as they fly.

▶ The house martin often lives near people, making its nest under the eaves of buildings, bridges, or other structures.

🔸 **There is an old saying** that the weather will be good when swallows fly high, but bad when swallows fly low. This is based on fact —in wet weather, insects stay nearer the ground, so the swallows do the same.

🔸 **An adult swallow** will carry a mass of crushed insects, squashed into a ball in its throat, back to its young. A barn swallow may take 400 meals a day to its chicks.

🔸 **The sand martin** digs a 50-in-long nesting burrow in riverbanks.

🔸 **Only discovered in 1968,** the white-eyed river martin spends the winter in reedbeds on Lake Boraphet in Thailand.

- **Purple martins** often nest in old woodpecker holes or in nestboxes. The female incubates the four to five eggs alone, but the male helps feed the young.

- **Sand martins** breed in the Northern Hemisphere, migrating south in the winter in flocks of thousands.

▼ *Swallows may lay up to eight eggs at a time, often in "mud cups" attached to buildings.*

# Larks

*▶ The skylark sings loudly over open countryside and is more often heard than seen.*

- **There are over 90 species** of lark, which live mainly in Africa, Europe, and Asia. More than half of all lark species are found in Africa.

- **Larks have more elaborate calls** than most birds and are famous for their complex, beautiful songs, which males use to defend their breeding territories and attract mates.

- **The skylark** performs a beautiful song as it flutters up to a great height, hovers, and descends again.

- **The female skylark** makes a shallow, grassy nest on the ground, and incubates three to four eggs.

- **Larks spend most of their time** hopping along the ground and most species have long back claws, which help them to balance.

- **Most larks** have dull, streaked-brown feathers, which gives them good camouflage on the ground, especially on the nest.

- **The shore lark** has the widest distribution of any lark. Its habitats range from the icy Arctic to deserts.

- **The shore lark** is the only member of the family to live in the Americas.

- **The thick-billed lark** has a larger, stronger beak than most larks, and uses it to crush hard seeds and tough-shelled insects.

- **The desert lark's** coloration varies according to where it lives—birds in areas of white sand have pale feathers, while those that live on dark volcanic sand are almost black.

▶ Also called the horned lark, the shore lark is found in the far north of Europe, as well as in North America, North Africa, and Asia.

# Wagtails and pipits

- **The wagtail family** has about 60 species, most of which are small, insect-eating birds. They include pipits and longclaws.

- **Wagtails and pipits** are mostly small, slender birds, with long tails and long legs. All species have long toes and often long claws, particularly the back toe.

- **Most wagtails** have a long, slim bill, but longclaws have a tougher bill to deal with the strong bodies of the beetles they feed on.

- **Wagtails are named** after their habit of flicking their tails up and down, which may tell neighboring wagtails to keep out of their territory.

◀ *Although the plumage of pied wagtails is black-and-white, the actual patterns and depth of color varies over the year. Females have more gray than black feathers.*

**DID YOU KNOW?**
Pied wagtails are often mistaken for young magpies, but they can be distinguished by their bouncing tails.

◀▶ *The rock pipit (left) is larger and darker than the meadow pipit (right), with a more heavily streaked breast, a longer bill and darker legs.*

🦋 **Wagtails have more striking colors** than pipits, but their songs are mostly quiet, whereas pipits have loud songs.

🦋 **The golden pipit** and the longclaws live on the savanna grasslands in Africa. They show off their colored underparts during their displays.

🦋 **The cape longclaw** from southern Africa has a catlike alarm call as well as a variety of whistling and piping calls. It rises some 33 ft into the air during its display flight.

🦋 **The rock pipit** feeds partly on the insects living in rotting seaweed along beaches. It also eats shellfish, small crustaceans, and seashore plant food.

🦋 **Craneflies** are one of the favorite foods of the meadow pipit. Adults may feed their chicks on craneflies for two weeks. The chicks develop in a nest of dry grass lined with down.

# Weavers and relatives

- **The cuckoo weaver** is a small, yellow bird that lays its eggs in the nests of grass warblers, leaving the warblers to raise its young.

- **Desert-living sociable weavers** use their nests all year round to shelter from sun, wind, and cold. At night, when temperatures drop, the nest holes stay considerably warmer than the outside.

- **Most weavers** have short, strong beaks that they use for feeding on seeds and insects.

- **The baya weaver** makes a beautiful nest of woven grass and leaves, which it hangs from a tree or roof.

- **The red-vented malimbe** (a weaver) feeds mainly on the husks of oil palm nuts.

- **Whydah birds** do not make their own nests, but lay their eggs in the nests of other birds, usually waxbills.

- **Young whydahs** make the same sounds and have the same mouth markings as their foster parents' own young, and because of this they get fed.

▶ When a male cape weaver has finished making a nest, it calls to a female.

◀ The male paradise whydah shows off his long tail feathers to impress a female or warn off rivals.

🦋 **In the breeding season**, the male paradise whydah grows 11-in-long tail feathers—almost twice the length of its body—for display in flight.

🦋 **The red bishop** mates with three or four females, who all nest in his territory.

▶ The male bishop bird has bright red and black plumage in the breeding season. For the rest of the year, his feathers are a streaky brown color.

# Fairy-wrens and relatives

- **The 26 species of fairy-wrens** live in Australia and New Guinea, where they forage for insects on the ground.

- **Young fairy-wrens** often stay with their parents and help them raise the next brood of young. Pairs with helpers can raise more young than those without.

- **During its courtship display**, the male superb fairy-wren may present his mate with a yellow flower petal.

- **If a predator** comes too close to a fairy-wren's nest, the parent birds make a special "rodent run" away from the nest, squeaking and trailing their tails to confuse and distract the enemy.

- **The rockwarbler** makes its nest in a dark cave or mine shaft and attaches it to the walls with spiderwebs.

▶ *The white-throated gerygone belongs to the Australasian warbler family, found in Australia, New Zealand, and adjacent islands.*

▶ *Male splendid fairy wrens have shiny, bright-blue feathers in the breeding season. Females are duller in color all year round.*

- **The 50 or so species of thickhead** live in rain forests and scrub in Southeast Asia and Australasia and have a whistling call.

- **The white-throated gerygone's nest** hangs from a eucalyptus branch and is made from bark strips and plant fibers woven together with spiderwebs.

- **The hooded pitohui** (thickhead family) is one of the very few poisonous birds known. Its feathers and skin contain a poison that protects it from predators. The poison comes from beetles that the bird eats.

- **The Australasian warbler family** includes 65 species of gerygone, thornbills, and scrubwrens.

- **The golden whistler** is probably the most variable of birds—the 70 or more races all have slightly different feather patterns or beak shapes.

# Parrots

There are over 370 species in the parrot group, including birds such as macaws, budgerigars, lories, and cockatoos. They live in Central and South America, Africa, southern Asia, and Australasia.

Parrots lay white eggs and their young are helpless when they hatch out.

The only flightless parrot is the New Zealand kakapo or owl parrot, which is now extremely rare.

▲ The male Australian king parrot is more brightly colored than the female, which is mainly green in color.

Unlike most parrots, the kea of New Zealand eats meat as well as fruit and insects. It feasts on carrion (animals that are already dead) and also hunts young shearwaters in their burrows.

The little blue-crowned hanging parrot gets its name from its strange habit of hanging upside down from a branch when at rest.

At about 33.5 in long, the scarlet macaw of South and Central America is one of the largest members of the parrot family.

The average lifespan of a scarlet macaw is 30–50 years, but they have been known to live for up to 75 years in captivity.

🦜 **Macaws nest** in tree holes high in rain forest trees. The female lays two eggs, which her mate helps to incubate. The young macaws stay with their parents for up to one year.

🦜 **Macaws swallow** beakfuls of clay from riverbanks. The clay may help to protect the birds from the effects of some plants and seeds that they eat, many of which are poisonous to other creatures.

▶ *With its bright red feathers, the scarlet macaw is one of the most beautiful of all the parrots. It can fly at up to 35 mph as it searches the rain forest for fruit, nuts, and seeds to eat.*

127

# Lories, lorikeets, and cockatoos

▲ *The galah is sometimes called the roseate cockatoo, because of its pink feathers. Pairs of galahs stay together for life and share the work of incubating the eggs and feeding the young.*

🦜 **Lories and lorikeets** feed mainly on pollen and nectar from flowering trees and shrubs, instead of feeding on seeds and fruits like other parrots.

🦜 **Lories and lorikeets** have long tongues with brushlike tips for mopping up their food.

🦜 **The bills of lories and lorikeets** are narrower, longer, and less powerful than those of other parrots, because they do not have to crush hard or tough foods.

- **Most species of lory and lorikeet** have to fly long distances in search of food. Rainbow lorikeets have been seen flying up to 50 mi between Pacific islands.

- **Lories are quarrelsome birds** with elaborate threat displays, such as fluttering, bobbing, and bouncing.

- **Cockatoos** have movable crests of feathers on their heads and narrow, stubby tongues.

- **The largest cockatoo**, and the largest Australian parrot, is the palm cockatoo. As part of his courtship display, the male holds a stick in his foot and drums loudly against a tree trunk.

- **The sulfur-crested cockatoo** is an all-white parrot with a yellow crest.

- **Australia's smallest cockatoo** is the cockatiel. It is the only cockatoo with a long, pointed tail.

▶ The palm cockatoo is also called the goliath cockatoo, because of its large size. It can grow up to 23 in long. This large parrot uses its powerful bill to crack open hard nuts and seeds.

# Warblers

- **The warbler family** has more than 380 species. Most live in Europe, Africa, Asia, and Australasia, but there are a few species in North and South America.

- **Typical warblers** are small birds, with fine, narrowly pointed bills. They have strong feet, which are well-suited to perching.

- **Most warblers** are 3.5–6.3 in long, but the two largest—the South African grassbird and the Australian songlarks—are up to 9 in long.

- **Insects** are the main food of most warblers, but they also eat some fruits, berries, and seeds.

▶ At 7.5 in long, the great reed warbler is larger than most European warblers.

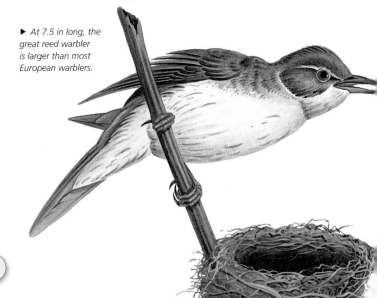

◀▶ *The willow warbler (left) is plumper than the chiffchaff (right), with more yellow underparts and paler legs. The chiffchaff has dark legs.*

🪶 **Chiffchaffs and willow warblers** look almost exactly alike, but their songs are quite different.

🪶 **The willow warbler** is only 4.3 in long, but it flies all the way from northern Europe and Siberia to Africa to spend the winter. This is a distance of some 7,500 mi.

DID YOU KNOW?

The rarely seen grasshopper warbler has an extraordinary whirring song and can "throw its voice" like a ventriloquist.

🪶 **The grasshopper warbler** has an extra-long middle toe, which enables it to hold two plant stems at once when it moves through tangled vegetation.

🪶 **The Aldabra brush warbler**, discovered in 1967, used to live on the Aladabra coral atoll in the Indian Ocean. It became extinct in 1986, possibly because cats, rats, and goats were introduced to the island.

🪶 **The barred warbler** has a harsh alarm call, but its song is rich and beautiful, rather like that of the nightingale.

🪶 **The blackcap** lays four to six eggs in a neat, cup-shaped nest. Both parents incubate them for ten to 15 days.

131

# More warblers

- **Sedge warblers** nest in hedges, reeds, coarse grass, or even cereal crops. They bind their cup-shaped nests firmly to plant stems.

- **Tree warblers** are larger and more heavily-built than most warblers. They have prominent legs and feet and often flick their tails.

- **In Europe**, the barred warbler often builds its nest near the ground, close to that of a red-backed shrike. This may help to protect its nest from predators.

- **The Dartford warbler** finds it difficult to survive the cold winters in Britain, but does not migrate to warmer climates.

- **If a willow warbler is disturbed** on her nest, she may pretend to be injured, fluttering away from the nest to lure predators away.

- **The tink-tink cisticola** builds its nest inside or beneath a grass tussock in southern Africa.

▶ *The secretive Dartford warbler has reddish-brown underparts. Young birds have paler plumage than the adults.*

- **The male zitting cisticola** climbs to a height of 115 ft or more during his song flight.

- **Goldcrests** may lay up to 13 eggs, which they incubate for 14–17 days. This is a relatively long incubation time for a perching bird.

**DID YOU KNOW?**

The goldcrest and the firecrest are only about 3.5 in long, and are Europe's smallest birds. The females make finely woven nests of lichen and cobwebs.

- **The spinifex bird** is a secretive warbler that rarely flies. Most of the time it hides on dense thickets of spinifex grass, which is common in the dry Australian grasslands.

- **Cuckoos lay their eggs** in the nests of many Fiji warblers, forcing the parents to raise the cuckoo chick as if it was their own.

▼ The male Eurasian goldcrest has an orange stripe on the crown of its head, whereas the female has a yellow stripe. During his courtship display, the male displays his crest to the female.

# Manakins and cotingas

🦜 **Manakins are small birds** that live in Central and South America. There are about 57 species.

🦜 **In his courtship display**, the male wire-tailed manakin brushes the female's chin with his long, wirelike tail feathers.

🦜 **Female manakins** do all the nesting work alone—they build the nest, incubate the eggs, and care for the young.

🦜 **Fruit and insects** are the main foods of both manakins and cotingas.

🦜 **The 65 or so cotinga species** live in the forests of Mexico, some Caribbean islands, and Central and South America.

🦜 **The largest of the cotingas** is the Amazonian umbrellabird, which gets its name from the crest of feathers that hangs over its head.

◄ *The little wire-tailed manakin lives in the lower levels of the Amazonian rain forest.*

**DID YOU KNOW?**

The female lovely cotinga destroys her nest after the young leave. This may help to stop predators finding the nest site, which is used year after year.

🐦 **The three-wattled bellbird** (cotinga family) is famous for its loud, explosive calls, which can be heard up to 2,600 ft away. It is named after the three black, wormlike wattles that hang from the sides of its mouth.

🐦 **Two of the most colorful South American birds** are the Guianan cock-of-the-rock, which is orange, and the Andean cock-of-the-rock, which is red (both cotinga family).

🐦 **The female cock-of-the-rock** makes a nest of mud and plants attached to a rock or cave wall, and incubates her eggs alone.

▼ *Male cock-of-the-rocks have brilliant red heads and shoulders. They perform complex display dances to females during the breeding season.*

135

# Tyrant flycatchers

- **The tyrant flycatcher family** comprises between 370 and 395 species of birds. They range from northern Canada, through the U.S., to the tip of South America.

- **Not all flycatchers** feed only on insects. The great kiskadee dives into water for fish and tadpoles, as well as catching flying insects in the air.

▲ *The vermilion flycatcher brings a flash of color to the desert and dry scrub of southwestern U.S., Central America, and tropical South America.*

- **The boat-billed flycatcher** has a larger beak than other flycatchers. It eats frogs and other small animals, as well as insects.

- **The vermilion flycatcher** is one of the few brightly colored flycatchers. The male has bright red plumage, which he shows off in his courtship display.

- **In 1976, ornithologists** (scientists who study birds) found a previously unknown flycatcher, which they named the cinnamon-breasted tody-tyrant. It lives only in cloud forests on a few mountain peaks in Ecuador and Peru.

**DID YOU KNOW?**
In the Galápagos Islands, vermilion flycatchers often perch on the backs of giant tortoises, so they can snap up the insects disturbed by their huge feet.

▲ The tyrant flycatchers are the largest bird family in North and South America. Shown here are:
1 buff-breasted flycatcher,
2 lesser flycatcher, and
3 great-crested flycatcher.

- **The royal flycatcher** is a plain, brownish bird, but it has an amazing crest of feathers on its head that it sometimes unfurls and shows off. Males have red crests and females have yellow or orange crests.

- **Smallest of all the tyrant flycatchers** is the short-tailed pygmy tyrant, at only 2.6 in long. It lives in northern South America.

- **The eastern phoebe** makes a nest of mud mixed with grass and plant stems. The female lays three to seven eggs, and incubates them for 14–16 days. The young leave the nest when they are about 17 days old.

- **Some flycatchers**, including the great crested flycatcher, line their nests with snakeskins that have been cast off.

# Old World flycatchers

🍃 **There are 147 species of Old World flycatchers**. Some live in wooded parts of Europe, but they are more common in Asia, Africa, and Australasia.

🍃 **The spotted flycatcher** sits on a branch watching for insect prey, then darts out to catch it in midair. It has been seen catching one insect every 18 seconds.

🍃 **Male spotted flycatchers** provide all the food for their brood when they first hatch. Later, both parents feed the chicks.

🍃 **The rufous-bellied niltava** lives and breeds in the Himalayas at altitudes of up to 7,500 ft.

🍃 **Pied flycatchers** usually nest in holes in old trees, but will also nest in nest boxes put up by people. Their nest hole is between one and 50 ft above the ground.

🍃 **In the fall and during winter**, the pied flycatcher eats worms and berries as well as insects.

▶ The spotted flycatcher lives in woodland, parks, and yards in Europe and parts of Asia and Africa.

▲ *Some Old World flycatchers have dull brown plumage. This male narcissus flycatcher has a bright yellow breast, but the female is plainer.*

🦋 **After a summer in Europe**, the red-breasted flycatcher flies to India and Southeast Asia for the winter.

🦋 **The female red-breasted flycatcher** makes a cup-shaped nest of moss, leaves, spiders' webs, and plant down, in which to lay her five to six eggs.

🦋 **The white-throated jungle flycatcher** is now very rare and lives only on two islands in the Philippines.

🦋 **Instead of catching all its food in the air**, the Australian flame robin often pounces onto its prey from a low perch.

▶ *The male Japanese blue flycatcher attracts a mate using his brilliant blue feathers and complex, trilling song. These flycatchers migrate to Japan for the warmer spring and summer months, nesting and feeding in woodlands, yards, and parks.*

139

# Vireos and relatives

- **The 43 species of vireo** live in North, Central, and South America, and range in size from 4–6 in.

- **Insects** such as caterpillars and aphids are the main foods of vireos, but some species also eat fruit.

- **When vireos were first named** in the 1800s, people thought they heard the word "vireo," meaning "I am green," in the birds' song. In fact most vireos are green.

◀▼ *Different species of vireo often live alongside each other in their forest habitats by feeding at different levels.*

**Yellow-throated vireo**

**Chestnut-sided shrike vireo**

◄ The red-eyed vireo breeds in North America in the summer.

🦋 **Vireos take about a week** to make their nests. The female makes a cup-shape of spiders' webs and silkworm threads around her body, and then adds plant material such as grass and moss.

🦋 **The black-capped vireo** usually attaches its nest to a forked twig. Both parents incubate the three to five eggs and feed the young.

🦋 **Red-eyed vireo chicks** are naked and helpless when they hatch, but open their eyes after four to five days, and leave the nest after 12 days.

🦋 **Plantcutters** get their name from their large, serrated beaks, used to chop leaves from plants.

🦋 **The three species of plantcutter** live in southern South America. The birds are 7–8 in long.

🦋 **The sharpbill** of Central and South America picks tiny insects and spiders from leaves.

🦋 **The brown-headed cowbird** often lays its eggs in the nests of vireos, which sometimes throw out the cowbird's eggs.

141

# Nuthatches

- **The 24 or so species of nuthatch** live in North America, Europe, north Africa, Asia, and Australasia.

- **Nuthatches** make the entrance to their nest hole smaller by plastering it in with mud, which dries to create a rock-hard surface.

- **Insects and spiders** are the main food of nuthatches, but in the fall the birds store nuts and seeds for the winter.

- **A nuthatch** wedges nuts, such as acorns, into crevices in tree bark and then hammers them open with its chisel-like bill.

- **The largest nuthatch** is the giant nuthatch, which is up to 7.8 in long.

- **The red-breasted nuthatch** paints the entrance of its tree hole nest with sticky pine resin. This may stop insects and other creatures getting into the nest, but the birds also have to take care not to get their own feathers stuck.

▲ A Eurasian nuthatch takes a nut from a garden bird feeder.

- **Red-breasted nuthatches** sometimes store the seeds from conifer tree cones as a food supply to last them through the winter.

- **The Eurasian nuthatch's** six to nine eggs hatch after 14–18 days.

- **Eurasian nuthatches** usually nest in old woodpecker holes near the tops of tall trees. They line the nest hole with flakes of bark and lichens.

- **The Kabylie nuthatch** digs its own nest holes in soft and rotten wood.

▼ Most nuthatches stay in the same area all year round. Some northerly populations of red-breasted nuthatches migrate south when there are not enough cone seeds to eat or their numbers grow too large.

▲ The white-breasted nuthatch lives in North American woodlands. It often starts searching for food high in a tree and crawls down it head first, clinging on tightly with its strong claws.

# Treecreepers

- **There are seven species** of treecreeper, seven species of Australian creeper, and two species of Philippine creeper.

- **A treecreeper** supports itself with its stiff tail feathers as it moves up tree trunks, feeding on insects and spiders.

- **The common treecreeper** cannot move down a tree trunk. It begins its search for insects low down on one tree, climbs up the tree in a spiral, and then flies to the base of another tree to start all over again.

- **The nest of a common treecreeper** is usually behind loose bark or ivy on old trees, or in large cracks in a tree trunk.

- **When the chicks of a common treecreeper** hatch out, both parents feed them for about two weeks.

◀ The common treecreeper lives in woodland, parks, and yards in Europe and Asia.

- **Young common treecreepers** can climb well when they leave the nest, but are not very good at flying.

- **The spotted gray creeper** of Africa and India does not have a stiffened tail. Like a nuthatch, it can run down, as well as up, trees.

- **The plain-headed creeper** from the Philippines searches leaves and twigs in the tree canopy for its insect food. It also laps up forest nectar with its brush-tipped tongue.

- **The red-browed treecreeper** of southeast Australia feeds mainly on ants. They live in family groups, with older young helping their parents to rear another brood of chicks.

▶ *The white-throated treecreeper is an Australian species that eats mainly insects, such as ants, probing under loose bark to find its prey.*

145

# Mockingbirds and relatives

▶ *The northern mockingbird is the best mimic in its family, usually copying the sounds made by other bird species.*

🐦 **Mockingbirds** are so-called because they imitate the calls of as many as 36 other bird species.

🐦 **As well as mockingbirds**, the 32 species in the family includes catbirds, thrashers, and tremblers. They live in North and South America.

🐦 **"Mimic of many tongues"** is the meaning of the northern mockingbird's scientific name, *Mimus polyglottus.*

🐦 **Some birds in the mockingbird family** and several other distantly related families are called catbirds because of their strange, catlike calls.

- **The gray catbird** migrates at night, arriving in the southern U.S. in spring after spending the winter in Central America.

- **The gray catbird** lines its cup-shaped nest of sticks, leaves, and grasses with pine needles and down. The female lays three to five eggs, and incubates them for 12–13 days.

- **The brown trembler**, a resident of some Caribbean islands, gets its name from its habit of shaking its body from time to time.

- **The brown thrasher** scatters dead leaves with its beak as it searches on the ground for its insect prey.

- **The 13 accentor species** live in mountainous parts of northern Africa, Europe, and Asia.

- **The dunnock** (accentor family) is a small brown bird. Its name comes from the Old English word *dunn*, meaning "dark or dull."

▼ *Brown thrashers are secretive birds. They look rather like thrushes, but are larger and have streaks (not spots) below.*

# Shrikes and vangas

**Red-backed shrike**

**Masked shrike**

**Northern shrike**

◄▲ *Shrikes often hunt from a perch, swooping down to catch insects or other prey in their strong bills. Northern shrikes (left) also hover in the air, ready to pounce on anything that moves.*

🦋 **There are about 70 species** of shrikes found in Africa, Europe, Asia, and North America, as well as 84 species of cuckoo shrikes and 14 species of helmet shrikes.

🦋 **All shrikes** have powerful hooked beaks that they use for killing insects, lizards, and frogs.

🦋 **Shrikes** are also known as "butcher birds," because of their habit of storing prey on the thorns and barbs of trees and bushes.

- **The yellow-billed shrike** lives in noisy groups of up to 15 individuals. All members of the group help to defend their territory and feed the female that lays the eggs, as well as her young when they hatch.

- **The fiscal shrike** is very aggressive—it sometimes kills other birds.

- **During its courtship display**, the male puffback (a shrike) fluffs up the long feathers on its lower back like a powder puff.

- **The call of the brubru shrike** sounds just like a phone ringing.

- **The loggerhead shrike** makes a nest of twigs and grass in a thorny bush or tree, where the female incubates between five and seven eggs.

  - **The sickle-billed vanga** uses its long, curved beak to probe bark for insects. It hangs upside down by its claws while it feeds.

    - **Most of the vanga shrikes** live in groups out of the breeding season, feeding and moving in loose flocks of up to 12 individuals.

◄ *The sickle-billed vanga is named after its long, curved beak.*

149

# Pittas and relatives

▶ Giant pittas are shy birds that live in the forests of Southeast Asia. They are threatened by the destruction of their forest habitat.

- **The brightly colored pittas** live in Africa, Southeast Asia, and Australia. *Pitta* is an Indian word meaning "bird"—it was first used in the 1700s.

- **The 26 or so species of pitta** range in size from 6–10 in. They are known for their use of tools, such as using a stone or a log to break open snail shells.

- **Pittas are said to have the best sense of smell** of any songbird. This may help them find worms and snails in the dim light of the forest floor.

- **The Indian pitta** makes a nest of moss and twigs. Both parents incubate the four to six eggs.

- **The four species of asity** are found only in Madagascar.

- **The wattled false sunbird** (asity family) gets its name from its long, sunbirdlike beak. Like the sunbirds, it takes nectar from flowers.

- **The broadbills** of tropical Africa and Southeast Asia are named after their flat bills, which have a very wide gape.

- **Most broadbills** feed on insects, which they catch in the air. Some also eat lizards and frogs.

- **The green broadbill** hangs its nest from a vine and covers it with lichen and spiders' webs.

DID YOU KNOW?

Rainbow pittas put wallaby droppings in and around their nests to disguise their own smell and keep tree snakes away from their eggs.

# Buntings

🍂 **More than three quarters** of all bunting species live in the Americas. There are about 60 species in North America alone.

🍂 **Buntings** have a stout, cone-shaped bill for crushing seeds and removing the husks around the outside. The top and bottom parts of the bill can be moved sideways in some species, such as juncos.

🍂 **Seeds are the main food** of the dark-eyed junco (bunting family), although it does eat a few spiders.

🍂 **Female buntings** usually incubate the eggs and look after the young, although the male shares the task of bringing food for the young.

🍂 **The little snow bunting** breeds in northern Greenland, further north than any other bird.

🍂 **Courtship displays** in snow buntings and lark buntings include a song flight, during which the birds rise a few feet above the ground and slowly circle back to the ground, holding their wings at an angle above their bodies.

🍂 **The Galápagos finches** (bunting family) are a group of closely related species. The similarities and difference between them were important evidence for Charles Darwin's theory of evolution.

◄ *Adult male snow buntings have black-and-white feathers in summer, but turn brown and white in winter.*

▲ The bright colors of the male painted bunting contrast with those of the green female, which is one of the few truly green birds in North America.

- **The male painted bunting** is the only bird with a blue head and red underparts.

- **The Lapland bunting** migrates to the Arctic tundra to nest in the summer months. These buntings often nest in small groups so they can warn each other of danger.

- **Lapland buntings** are also called Lapland longspurs, because of the long claws on their back toes, which help them to balance on the ground.

▶ Male yellowhammers have a bright-yellow head. They feed on the ground but sing loudly from a perch during the summer breeding season.

# Tanagers

- **The 240 species in the tanager family** include flowerpiercers, honeycreepers, and euphonias. All live in North and South America.

- **One tanager**, the glossy flowerpiercer, has a hooked, upward-curving beak that it uses to pierce the bases of tubular flowers so it can feed on the nectar inside.

- **The male scarlet tanager** has bright-red feathers in the breeding season, but in autumn its plumage changes to olive-green, similar to the female.

- **The western tanager** lines its nest of twigs and moss with fine roots and animal hair. The female incubates three to five eggs.

- **Some tanagers follow columns of army ants** in forests, and snap up the insects that flee the ants' path.

- **Western tanagers** nest in mountain forests, where the female builds the nest and incubates the eggs.

- **Western tanagers** migrate to Central America to find warmer weather during the winter.

- **Shrike tanagers** are good at catching flying insects in mid-air.

- **Shrike tanagers** sometimes give false alarm calls to trick their flock mates into hiding from a non-existent predator. This gives them a better chance of catching the available insects.

- **Groups of hooded mountain tanagers** feed together, calling loudly at dawn to tell other groups of tanagers where they are.

▶ Tanagers are a colorful group of birds that live in the mainly tropical forests of South America.

1 Thick-billed euphonia    5 Glistening green tanager
2 Summer tanager    6 Blue-gray tanager
3 Swallow tanager    7 Masked crimson tanager
4 Yellow-rumped tanager

# Bowerbirds

- **Male bowerbirds** build bowers of twigs and other plant material to attract females. They decorate their creations with berries and shells, and some even perform dances in front of their bowers.

- **Male bowerbirds' bowers** are not built as places for the female to lay eggs and rear young. The females build their own, more practical nests.

- **Bowerbirds** feed on fruit, berries, seeds, insects, and other small creatures.

▼ *A male satin bowerbird shows off his bower to a female. He has built the bower from two walls of sticks, forming an "avenue," and decorated the area around it with blue objects.*

**Spotted bowerbird**

**Fawn-breasted bowerbird**

**Masked bowerbird**

▲ The spotted bowerbird decorates his bower with piles of white and green objects, while the fawn-breasted bowerbird uses green berries. The masked bowerbird is among the most brightly colored of all bowerbirds.

🐾 **A female bowerbird** has between one and three chicks and cares for them alone.

🐾 **The Vogelkop gardener bowerbird** builds a hutlike structure big enough for a person to crawl into.

🐾 **The forests of New Guinea** and northern and eastern Australia are home to the 18 or so species of bowerbird.

🐾 **At about 14 in long**, the great gray bowerbird of northern Australia is the largest of the family.

🐾 **The male regent bowerbird** paints its bower yellow using a mix of spit and the juice of crushed leaves.

🐾 **The spotted catbird** is a member of the bowerbird family but the males do not build bowers and males and females look alike.

157

# Antbirds and tapaculos

▲ *Lines of army ants lead tropical antbirds to their food.*

- **Antbirds** follow columns of army ants as they march over the forest floor, perching just above the ground to seize other insects as they flee from the ants' path.

- **The 230 or so species of antbird** live in Mexico, Central, and South America.

- **Antbirds** mate for life.

- **During the courtship ritual** of the ocellated antbird, the male presents the female with an item of food.

- **Antbirds have white spots** on their back feathers, which they use to signal warnings to each other. They show the spots in particular patterns according to the message—like a sort of Morse code.

- **Antbird species** range from 4–15 in long, and have differently shaped beaks to suit their food.

- **Some larger species of antbirds** have a special "tooth" inside the beak that helps them chew food.

- **Most antbirds** do not fly much and have poorly developed wings, but their legs are strong for running and perching.

- **The 30 species of tapaculos** are insect-eating birds that live in the cool mountain forests of South America or in dry scrubland.

► The white-plumed antbird lives in the Amazon rain forest. Its long legs help to protect it from the ants' stings as it gathers up the other insects or spiders disturbed by the ants.

159

# Finches and relatives

🔖 **The crossbill** gets its name from its crossed beak, which is specially shaped for extracting seeds from pine cones.

🔖 **The beaks** of some crossbills cross to the left, while those of others cross to the right.

🔖 **The male American goldfinch** brings the female food while she incubates the four to six eggs.

🔖 **The kernels** of cherry stones and olive stones are a favourite food of the strong-beaked hawfinch.

🔖 **The goldfinch** uses its slender beak like tweezers to take seeds from between the spines of a teasel head.

🔖 **Young chaffinches** can fly just 12 days after hatching.

▶ *The distinctive, pink-breasted male bullfinch.*

▼ *The goldfinch has a red face, beige body, and a broad yellow bar on its black wings. A flock of goldfinches is called a "charm."*

- **The oriole finch** is named after its colors, which are similar to those of true orioles. It lives in the mountain forests of Africa.

**DID YOU KNOW?**
Although the hawfinch weighs only 1.8 oz, its beak can exert a pressure of 99 lb.

- **In winter**, when food becomes scarce, large flocks of different species of finches and tits search for food together.

- **Redpolls** are named after their red forehead, or "poll." Young birds have no red coloring and also have yellower bills than the adults.

- **The blue chaffinch** is a rare species, which lives only in the Canary Islands. Adults eat mainly seeds, but the young are fed on insects.

▼ The brightly colored male chaffinch brings insect food to the dull-colored female. The nest is a neat cup of grass, moss, and lichens, lined with soft hair.

161

# Hawaiian finches

- **Hawaiian finches** are also known as Hawaiian honeycreepers. They are small perching birds that are found only on the Hawaiian Islands.

- **Male Hawaiian finches**, or honeycreepers, are often more brightly colored than the females.

- **Scientists believe** that the 32 or so species of Hawaiian finches evolved from a sparrowlike bird that crossed more than 1,800 mi of ocean to reach the islands some 4–5 million years ago.

- **The Maui parrotbill** has a strong, finchlike bill, which it uses to crush or pull open the small branches of trees to reach the beetle grubs inside. It also eats caterpillars and other insects.

- **The Nukupuu** has a thin bill and feeds on nectar and insects. It has a tubelike tongue with a fringed tip that soaks up nectar.

- **The bright-red feathers** of the Iiwi were once used to make the feathered capes, helmets, and other ornaments of Hawaiian chiefs.

- **The Iiwi** makes a variety of interesting sounds, such as creaks, gurgles, whistles, and reedy notes.

- **The Akiapolaau** has a straight lower bill for hammering tree bark in search of insects, and a curved top bill to extract the insects from their hiding places.

- **The Palila** holds the pods of mamane trees in its feet and uses its heavy bill to rip them open and reach the seeds inside.

▶ *The Iiwi feeds mainly on flowering trees, probing the blossoms for nectar with its long bill, which curves downward.*

# Thrushes

- **There are about 173 species** of "true thrushes," which include the American robin, Eurasian blackbird, fieldfare, redwing, ring ouzel, and ground thrush.

- **Thrushes** are plump birds with soft plumage (feathers). They often feed on the ground.

- **Thrushes** have slender bills and feed primarily on insects, but most species also eat worms, snails, and fruit.

- **The songs** of some thrush species are very beautiful.

- **The lower legs** of thrushes are covered in front with one long scale instead of many short ones.

- **Most species of thrush** are gray or brown in color, often with speckled underparts. The young are usually spotted in their first plumage.

- **The American robin**—the largest of the North American thrushes—lives both in cities and mountains.

◀ The song thrush is named after its magnificent song. It is also known for its habit of using a large stone as an anvil to smash open snail shells.

▲ *The male Eurasian blackbird has black feathers, while the female is brown, with spots on her breast. Young blackbirds are the same color as females, but with more spots.*

**The female blackbird** makes a cup-shaped nest of plant stems, grass, twigs, and roots. The four to five eggs hatch after 11–17 days.

**Blackbirds** were taken to Australia and New Zealand in the 19th century. Their songs are now clearly different to blackbirds living in Europe.

**A number of unrelated birds**, such as antthrushes, babbling thrushes and laughing thrushes, are called thrushes because they look similar to true thrushes.

◄ *Fieldfares are noisy thrushes that eat insects, spiders, and centipedes, as well as seeds and fruit, such as apples and hawthorn berries. Parents will squirt droppings at predators to defend their young.*

165

# Chats and relatives

- **There are about 180** or so chats and relatives, such as the European robin, bush robins, stonechats, redstarts, wheatears, forktails, bush chats, rock thrushes, palm thrushes, shamas (magpie robins), and many small robins.

- **The chats** and their relatives used to be grouped with the thrushes, but are now grouped with the Old World flycatchers.

- **The wheatear breeds** in the Arctic, but in the fall flies some 2,000 mi to Africa, where it spends the winter.

- **The familiar orange-red breast** of a robin indicates that the bird is at least two months old.

- **Best known for its beautiful song**, the nightingale sings during the day as well as at night.

▼ *The male European robin sings to claim his feeding and breeding territory.*

▶ The drab-colored nightingale skulks in dense undergrowth in deciduous woodlands, sometimes darting out of its hiding place to snatch insects, such as beetles, from the ground.

🐾 **The redstart** is named after its bright-red tail—*steort* is Anglo-Saxon for "tail."

🐾 **The call of a stonechat** sounds like two pebbles being banged together.

🐾 **The white-crowned forktail** lives close to mountain streams in Asia. It hunts for insects along rocky stream banks or on the surface of the water.

🐾 **The male rock thrush** makes its piping or warbling song from a perch and also as it soars into the air on a display flight. It returns to the ground silently.

🐾 **Asian magpie robins** are common in towns and gardens, often nesting in buildings or under the eaves of houses.

# Babblers

🦅 **The only species** of the babbler family to live in North America is the wren-tit, while 256 species are found in Asia, Africa, and Australasia.

🦅 **The white-necked rockfowl** makes a mud nest on the roof of caves. It sometimes builds onto old wasps' nests.

🦅 **The tuneful song** of the red-billed leiothrix makes it a popular cage bird in China.

🦅 **Although common in west Africa**, the pale-breasted thrush-babbler is so good at hiding on the forest floor, where it searches for insects, that it is rarely seen.

🦅 **Brightly colored patches** of bare skin on the head are a distinguishing feature of rockfowl.

▼ *Male and female babblers raise their young together.*

▼ *The noisy blackcap babbler lives in flocks of up to 12 birds in the forests and scrubland of west Africa. It builds a cup-shaped nest in the trees and all the birds in a flock help to raise the young.*

**The grey-crowned babbler** lives in family groups of up to 12 individuals, which usually consists of a pair of babblers and their young from previous years.

**Flocks of common babblers** make musical whistling calls as they scuttle or hop through the undergrowth, searching for insects, grain, and berries.

**The tiny chestnut-headed fulvetta** is a babbler of high altitudes in the Himalayas, reaching heights of up to 13,000 ft.

**The whiskered yuhina** has a crest of feathers on its head. It often feeds in mixed flocks with other birds, singing all the time.

**Black-capped sibias** sometimes drink the sap oozing from holes in the trunks of oak trees, rather like North American sapsuckers.

# Wrens

- **The cactus wren** builds its dome-shaped nest among the spines of cacti in the deserts of North America. Few enemies will brave the spines to steal the wren's eggs or young.

- **At about 9 in long**, the black-capped donacobious of South America is the largest of the wren family.

- **A male wren** courts a mate by building up to 12 nests. The female chooses one in which to lay her eggs.

- **The northern (or winter) wren** usually lays between five and eight eggs, and incubates them for 14–17 days. The young stay in the nest for 20 days.

- **Most wrens** live in North and South America. Only the northern wren lives in Europe, Asia, and Africa.

- **The rock wren** survives in a harsh, rocky environment by eating small insects and worms. It has a brown rump.

- **The song of the flutist wren** consists of a series of high-pitched whistling notes and may last up to 30 seconds.

▶ These two North American wrens live in different habitats —the Carolina wren (top) is a bird of woodlands and rocky slopes, while the marsh wren (bottom) lives in reed marshes.

- **The tiny northern wren** can fly well but spends most of its time hopping and flitting over the ground or through bushes, probing for insects and spiders with its needle-sharp bill.

- **Male long-billed marsh wrens** build clusters of 25–35 nests over a breeding season of three months. Males sing near their nests and show them off to the females. However, the females breed in another nest away from the courtship area.

- **Cactus wrens** produce up to four broods of young every year.

▲ *Bewick's wren looks rather like a Carolina wren, but has a white breast and outer tail feathers, as well as a very different song.*

◄ *The cactus wren is the largest wren in North America, reaching lengths of 7–8.5 in. These active and curious wrens get almost all their water from their food, which includes insects, seeds, fruit, and some lizards and frogs.*

171

# Sunbirds and relatives

- **The 132 or so species of sunbird** live in tropical parts of Africa, Asia, and Australia.

- **Sunbirds** use their long, slender beaks and tubular tongues to extract sweet liquid nectar from flowers.

- **Female sunbirds** make purse-shaped nests for their two to three eggs, which hatch after 13–15 days.

- **The male pygmy sunbird** has long tail spikes and metallic feathers during the breeding season, but has a short tail and dull plumage at other times.

- **In order to attract a mate**, both male and female scarlet-tufted malachite sunbirds puff out red tufts of feathers on the front of their wings.

- **At about 9 in long**, the Sao Tomé giant sunbird is the largest of its family. It uses its hooked beak to dig into the bark of trees for insects.

- **The flowerpecker family** contains about 44 species living in parts of Asia, Southeast Asia, and Australia.

▶ Sunbirds feed from tropical flowers. They often hover as they do this, but cannot fly backward like hummingbirds.

**DID YOU KNOW?**
The mistletoe bird (flowerpecker family) swallows mistletoe berries whole, digesting only the flesh and not the seeds.

▼ *The striated pardalote nests in tree hollows, or at the end of a burrow dug in a cliff or riverbank. It lives in open forests and woodlands over most of Australia, and often searches for its insect food high in the branches of eucalyptus or wattle trees.*

- **Flowerpeckers** are small, stout, dumpy birds with short necks, legs, and tails. They range in size from the 4 in pygmy flowerpecker to the 7 in mottled flowerpecker.

- **The crested berrypecker** (flowerpecker family) has a habit of rubbing its plumage with crushed flower petals.

- **Flower nectar** is important in the diet of many flowerpeckers. They have short, thick, curved bills and tubular tongues to help them feed on nectar.

173

# Honeyeaters

- **Honeyeaters** are the most important flower pollinators in Australia. The brushlike tip on the honeyeater's tongue helps it to extract flower nectar.

- **The tui** of New Zealand is also known as the parson bird, because it has a distinctive bib of white feathers at its throat.

- **In the breeding season**, male tuis make spectacular dives to impress females. They zoom downward at high speed, rolling and looping-the-loop as they do so.

- **Blue-faced honeyeaters** are bold, inquisitive birds that raid banana plantations and eat syrup in fields of sugar cane.

- **Male and female honeyeaters** usually look the same, but the male cardinal honeyeater has bright red-and-black feathers, while the female is a dull green-grey with small red patches.

- **Groups of noisy friarbirds** often squabble over their food. They feed on the fruit and nectar of eucalypt and banksias trees in Australia and New Guinea.

◄ *A New Holland honeyeater gathers a supply of energy-rich nectar from a flower.*

◄ The white-cheeked honeyeater looks very similar to the New Holland honeyeater, but these two birds avoid competing with each other by perching in different places and nesting at different seasons.

🦤 **New Holland honeyeaters** help to spread the pollen of a wide range of Australian plants as they feed on the nectar from flowers.

🦤 **The western spinebill** sometimes hovers in front of flowers to drink the nectar, soaking it up with a brush at the tip of its tongue.

🦤 **Groups of up to 30 noisy miners** defend a nesting area and join together to mob (dive-bomb and attack) predators.

🦤 **The yellow wattlebird** is the largest of the honeyeaters. It was named after the bright-yellow wattles (fleshy strips) that hang down from its cheeks.

▶ Black honeyeaters, especially females, are sometimes called charcoal birds, because they often eat charcoal and ash at old camp fires. They live in drier parts of Australia.

175

# Lyrebirds and relatives

- **The two species of lyrebird** live in dense mountain forest in southeastern Australia.

- **In its loud song**, the lyrebird may imitate other birds, barking dogs, chainsaws, and even passing trains.

- **The female lyrebird** builds a domed nest, usually close to the ground. Her single chick stays with her for eight months or more.

- **One of the biggest of all the songbirds**, the superb lyrebird has an extraordinary lyre-shaped tail, with feathers more than 20 in long.

▶ *During his courtship display, the male superb lyrebird fans out his long tail and arches it forward over his head to form a shimmering curtain. He does not build a nest or take care of the young.*

▶ The tiny New Zealand rifleman uses its large feet to grip tree trunks as it probes for insects in the tree bark with its thin, pointed bill. The rifleman belongs to an ancient family of New Zealand birds with no close relatives anywhere else in the world.

- **Young male superb lyrebirds** do not grow their lyre-shaped tails until they are three or four years old.

- **The two species of scrub-bird** live in Australia, where they feed on insects, lizards, and frogs.

- **Male scrub birds** have powerful, ringing calls, which can be heard from a long distance away in dense scrub.

- **The rufous scrub-bird** spends most of its time on the ground and rarely flies.

- **A full-grown rufous scrub-bird** is 6–8 in long and weighs about one ounce.

- **The rifleman**, one of the three species of New Zealand wrens, lays eggs that are about 20 percent of her body weight. She and the male recruit helpers to bring food to their young.

# Ovenbirds and relatives

▶ *The red-billed scythebill is easily distinguished by its long, downward-curving beak.*

🪶 **Ovenbirds** live in the forests, mountains, and semideserts of Mexico, Central, and South America.

🪶 **The nest of the firewood-gatherer** (ovenbird family) looks like a bonfire. A group of birds make the nest together and sleep in it during the winter.

🪶 **The common miner** (an ovenbird) digs a 10-ft-long burrow with a nest chamber at the end, where it raises its chicks and roosts for the rest of the year.

🪶 **Des Murs' wiretail** (an ovenbird) has only six tail feathers, four of which may be three times the length of its own body.

🪶 **The campo miner** (an ovenbird) nests in a very particular place— an old armadillo burrow.

🪶 **The 50 or so species of woodcreeper** live in forests and woodland in Mexico, Central, and South America.

- **Woodcreepers** often nest in old woodpecker nests.

- **The red-billed scythebill** (a woodcreeper) has a long, curved beak for delving deep into rain forest plants, such as ferns and bromeliads, to search for insects.

- **Red-billed scythebills** use their stiff tail feathers for support on tree trunks, rather like woodpeckers. They also cling onto the bark with their strong feet.

**DID YOU KNOW?**

The barred woodcreeper of Central and South America follows army ants as they march across the rain forest floor, snatching up insects trying to escape from the advancing army.

▶ The rufous hornero is the national bird of Argentina.

179

# Old World sparrows

- **Most sparrows** are about 5.5–7 in long and have brownish or gray plumage.

- **The 40 or so species of Old World sparrow** live in Europe, Africa, and parts of Asia. Some have been introduced elsewhere.

- **Chestnut sparrows** drive other birds from their nests and use the nests themselves, instead of making their own.

- **The snow finch** lives high in mountain ranges and makes its nest on mountain ledges at altitudes of 16,400 ft.

- **The desert sparrow** makes a nest of grass and twigs, often in a wall, and lays between two and five eggs.

- **The house sparrow** originally came from Southwest Asia, but has spread throughout the world. It feeds mainly on seeds, but also eats some insects and scraps put out on bird tables.

▶ The cape sparrow is a common bird around farms, towns, and yards in South Africa. The male (shown here) has a black head and throat, while the female is a gray colour.

▲ The male house sparrow has a gray crown and black bib. The female is a duller brown color with less distinct white wing bars. House sparrows have a conical bill for eating seeds, but are adaptable and intelligent birds that will feed on almost any food in towns and cities.

**DID YOU KNOW?**

Sparrows like to bathe and splash in water, and will even bathe in snow in winter.

🦅 **House sparrows** rarely nest away from human habitation.

🦅 **The house sparrow** was introduced into Brooklyn, New York, in 1851, and San Francisco and Salt Lake City in the 1870s. It is now common across all of North America except Alaska and far northern Canada.

🦅 **One pair of house sparrows** may raise an average of 20 chicks in a breeding season. They have a very short incubation period of between ten and 12 days.

181

# Drongos and relatives

- **The greater racquet-tailed drongo** has two long, wirelike tail feathers with twisted tips that make a humming noise as the bird flies.

- **The pied currawong** (Australian butcherbird family) attacks other birds and takes their young from their nests.

- **The 25 species of Old World oriole** live in Europe and parts of Asia, Africa, and Australia. They are mainly tree-dwellers, feeding on insects, seeds, and fruit.

- **The golden oriole** makes a neat, cup-shaped nest that it binds to two supporting twigs. It lays three to four eggs.

◄ The black-headed oriole builds a hanging nest in a tree, woven partly from fresh green grass. This shy American bird travels in pairs, even out of the nesting season.

▶ The greater racquet-tailed drongo has a plume of feathers on its head and long, vinelike tail streamers.

- **The figbird** (oriole family) is a forest fruit-eater, but is now also common in towns.

- **There are two surviving species** of New Zealand wattlebirds—the kokako and the saddleback. The saddleback lives only on offshore islands that have been cleared of predators.

- **The huia**, a species of wattlebird from New Zealand, is now extinct.

- **Australia and New Guinea** are home to the ten species of insect-eating bell-magpies.

- **Australian mud-nesters** work together to build nests of mud on the branches of trees.

- **Wood swallows**, found in Australasia and Southeast Asia, feed mostly on insects, but also drink nectar.

183

# Waxwings and relatives

- **The waxwing** gets its name from the red markings at the tips of its wing feathers, which look like drops of wax.

- **Adult waxwings** eat mainly berries, but feed their young on insects for the first two weeks of their lives.

- **There are three species** of waxwings. They are all sociable, tree-dwelling birds.

- **The bohemian waxwing** makes a nest of twigs, moss, and grass, usually in a conifer tree. The female incubates four to six eggs, while the male keeps her fed.

- **Adult cedar waxwings** store berries in their crops, or throat pouches, and regurgitate them for their young.

- **The single species of palmchat** is found on the islands of Hispaniola, Saona, and Gonâve in the Caribbean.

- **Palmchats** nest in palm trees. One nest may house 30 pairs of birds, each with its own tunnel entrance.

- **The silky flycatcher** feeds mostly on mistletoe berries, passing out the seeds.

- **Long-tailed silky flycatchers** build a nest of lichens. Both adults incubate the eggs and feed the young.

**DID YOU KNOW?**
Courting waxwings pass small objects, such as berries, flower petals, or insects, back and forth.

▶ Bohemian waxwings
will strip a bush clean of its
berries before moving on.

# Wood warblers

◀ The yellow warbler can be found from chilly Alaska to tropical South America.

🦜 **The 118 species of wood warbler** live in North, Central, and South America. They are also called New World warblers.

🦜 **All the wood warblers** are fairly small birds. The smallest species is the Lucy's warbler, which is just over 4 in.

🦜 **Most wood warblers** live and feed in trees, where they use their delicate bills to catch insects.

🦜 **Male wood warblers** usually develop bright colors and patterns in the breeding season, whereas females are drab colors.

🦜 **Many wood warblers**, such as blackpoll warblers, migrate long distances to spend the winter months in warm tropical areas.

- **Kirtland's warbler** has very specialized breeding needs—it nests only around jack pine trees that are up to 20 ft tall.

- **The maximum lifespan** of the magnolia warbler in the wild is about seven years.

- **Male cerulean warblers** are very aggressive in the breeding season. They attack each other with their feet and bills, while falling through the trees with their wings and tail spread.

- **Cowbirds** lay their eggs in magnolia warbler nests and the young cowbirds may push the warbler eggs and young out of the nest.

- **Ovenbirds** raise their crests when threatened to startle predators by showing the orange color on the crown of their heads.

▼ *The American redstart is one of the most common birds in North America. It flashes its orange-and-black wings and tail to startle insect prey out of hiding places in its woodland habitat.*

# American blackbirds and relatives

- **The Icterid family** contains nearly 100 species of American birds, including blackbirds, the bobolink, the meadowlarks, oropendolas, grackles, orioles, and cowbirds.

- **The male red-winged blackbird** sings and flashes its brightly colored "shoulder pads" to defend its breeding territory.

- **The bobolink** breeds in southern Canada and the U.S., and migrates to South America for the winter—the longest migration journey of any icterid.

- **The crested oropendola** weaves a hanging nest that may be up to 3 ft long. The birds nest in colonies, and there may be as many as 100 large hanging nests in one tree.

▼ Common grackles have highly iridescent plumage. They may seem to have black, blue, purple, green, or bronze feathers, depending on the light. They are very common near houses and homes, and form large, noisy roosts containing thousands of birds.

▶ The male northern oriole, also known as the Baltimore oriole, has vibrant orange and black plumage. The female is a duller olive-brown with orange or whitish underparts.

- **The largest of the 92 species** of icterid is the olive oropendola, which measures 20 in long.

- **Male icterids** are generally much larger than females. The male great-tailed grackle is as much as 60 percent heavier than the female.

- **Great-tailed grackles** are big, noisy birds that scavenge on rubbish as well as feeding on insects, grain, and fruit. They are common in towns and villages.

- **Male great-tailed grackles** do not look after their young, except to protect them from predators.

- **The Baltimore oriole** is the state bird of Maryland. A song named after the bird was written by Hoagy Carmichael in the 1930s.

- **Like the cuckoo**, the female brown-headed cowbird lays her eggs in the nests of other birds. She lays about 12–15 eggs a year.

# Bulbuls and relatives

- **There are about 120 species of bulbul** found in Africa and southern Asia, usually in forests, although some bulbuls have adapted to built-up areas.

- **Bulbuls** range in size from 5.5–10 in, and eat mainly insects and fruit.

- **The bearded greenbul** lives in African rain forests and has a beautiful whistling call, that it uses to keep in touch with others of its species in the dense jungle.

- **Despite its small size**, the red-vented bulbul is an aggressive bird. In Asia, people sometimes bet on a male bird to win a fight against another male.

- **The yellow-vented bulbul** makes a nest of twigs, leaves, and vine stems, often in a garden or on a balcony. Both parents incubate the two to five eggs and care for the young.

- **The two species of fairy bluebirds** live in Asia, feeding on fruit, nectar, and some insects.

▶ The fairy bluebird spends most of its time in trees, feeding on nectar and ripe fruit, especially figs.

▲ The red-whiskered bulbul is a common sight in gardens and cultivated land in India, south China, and Southeast Asia.

🪶 **Male fairy bluebirds** have bright-blue upperparts. Females are a dull greenish-blue with dark markings.

🪶 **Leafbirds** lay two to three eggs in a cup-shaped nest made in the trees.

🪶 **The common iora** (a leafbird) scurries through trees searching for insects. It sometimes eats mistletoe and other berries.

DID YOU KNOW?
When courting, the male common iora fluffs up its feathers, leaps into the air, and tumbles back to its perch again.

191

# Tits and chickadees

- **There are about 50 species of true tits** found in Europe, Africa, Asia, and North America. In addition, there are seven species of long-tailed tits and ten species of penduline tits.

- **The largest of the tits** is the Asian sultan tit, at about 8.5 in long and one ounce in weight. It is twice the size of most other tits.

- **The blue tit** is only 4–4.5 in long, but lays as many as 15 eggs—more than any other bird that feeds its young.

- **The penduline tit** makes an amazing nest woven from plant fibers suspended from the end of a twig. The walls of the nest may be one inch thick.

- **The black-capped chickadee** gets its name from its call, which sounds like a "chick-a-dee-dee," and is one of the most complex of any bird songs.

- **The female great tit** lays eight to 13 eggs, each of which is about 10 percent of her body weight.

- **Great tits** hatch blind and helpless, and are fed by their parents for about three weeks. The parents may make 1,000 feeding trips a day to the young.

◀ Black-capped chickadees are tame and inquisitive birds that often cling upside down to twigs and branches as they search for insects to eat.

▶ Both male and female penduline tits weave their purselike nest from grass, leaves, lichens, and moss. It takes about two weeks for them to build the nest, which keeps the chicks warm for two to three weeks while they grow their feathers.

The long-tailed tit makes its nest from feathers and moss that it collects—one nest may contain as many as 2,000 feathers.

The long-tailed tit is only about 5.5 in long, and more than half of its length is its tail feathers.

**DID YOU KNOW?**

The willow tit may bury up to 1,000 nuts and seeds a day, to eat later when food is scarce.

# Birds of paradise

🐦 **Birds of paradise**, of which there are about 44 species, live only in New Guinea and northeastern Australia.

🐦 **The king of Saxony bird of paradise** has two 20-in-long head plumes decorated with small, sky-blue squares. They look so unusual that they were first thought to be fake.

🐦 **The magnificent riflebird** gets its name from its loud whistling call, which sounds like a passing bullet.

🐦 **Most female birds of paradise** make a cup or dome-shaped nest, and lay one or two eggs.

◀ The male king bird of paradise uses its long, wirelike tail feathers in its courtship display.

DID YOU KNOW?
The tail feathers of the male ribbon-tailed bird of paradise are up to 3.3 ft long

194

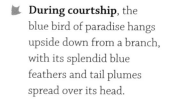

▲ *The blue bird of paradise is a rare member of this exotic family. It is threatened by the destruction of its forest habitat.*

🦃 **During courtship**, the blue bird of paradise hangs upside down from a branch, with its splendid blue feathers and tail plumes spread over its head.

🦃 **Fruit and insects** are the main foods of the birds of paradise. Some also eat leaves and buds.

🦃 **New Guinea tribesmen** traditionally wear bird of paradise feathers in their head`dresses.

🦃 **During the early 19th century**, 100,000 bird of paradise skins were sold each year in Europe for hat and dress decorations.

🦃 **The first bird of paradise skins** brought to Europe from New Guinea did not have feet, so some people thought the birds never landed.

195

# Starlings

🔖 **There are about 113 species** of starling in Europe, Africa, and Asia. Starlings have also been introduced into Australasia and North America.

🔖 **The largest starlings** are over 12 in long and weigh over 8 oz.

🔖 **Male starlings** bring fresh green leaves to the nest while the eggs are incubating. The leaves help the nestlings to cope with bird parasites, such as lice.

🔖 **European starlings** feed their young on caterpillars, earthworms, and beetle grubs, and may make 400 feeding trips a day.

▼ *A greater blue-eared glossy starling carries some nesting material to its nest in a tree hole. This starling lives in Africa.*

◄ *The male starling has glossy, iridescent plumage. The female is much plainer, with brownish feathers.*

🐦 **The male wattled starling** loses his head feathers in the breeding season. Scientists investigating cures for human baldness are researching the bird's ability to regrow its head feathers each year.

🐦 **When kept in captivity**, hill mynahs mimic human speech, but in the wild they do not imitate the calls of other bird species, only the calls of other hill mynahs.

🐦 **The Brahminy starling** has a brushlike tip on its tongue, used for collecting pollen and nectar.

🐦 **One hundred starlings** were released in New York in the 1890s. Today more than 200 million starlings live in North America.

🐦 **Locusts are the favorite food** of the rose-colored starling. Large flocks fly to wherever they are plentiful.

DID YOU KNOW?
In some cities, flocks of up to one million starlings gather for the night.

# Monarchs and relatives

🦜 **Monarch flycatchers** feed mainly on insects, darting out to catch them in the air and then taking them back to a perch to eat.

🦜 **The male** African paradise flycatcher's tail feathers are up to 8 in long—much longer than its body.

▲ The paradise flycatcher makes a neat nest of lichens and plant roots, held together with spiders' webs, on a slender branch or twig.

🦜 **The yellow-breasted boatbill**, a monarch flycatcher, has a broad beak with a hooked tip, which it uses to pick small insects off leaves.

🦜 **The male yellow-breasted boatbill** builds most of the nest, using vine tendrils to hang it from a fork in a tree branch.

🦜 **According to aboriginal folklore**, the willie wagtail (a fantail), is a gossipy bird that spreads secrets.

🦜 **During the breeding season**, willie wagtails are very aggressive and will attack much larger predators.

🦜 **The pied fantail's beak** is ringed with bristles that may help the bird to trap insect prey.

- **The white-browed fantail** flicks its wings and tail to disturb insects from crevices in old tree bark.

- **The black-naped blue monarch** lays three to four eggs in a nest of grass and bark, bound together with spiders' webs. The nest is usually built on a forked branch.

- **Black-naped blue monarchs** take insect prey back to a perch and hold it under one foot as they break it into pieces.

▼ *The Asian black-naped blue monarch is an active bird, always flicking its wings and fanning its tail. These small flycatchers are sociable birds but have no real song.*

# Birds of prey
# and owls

# What is a bird of prey?

- **Birds of prey** hunt other animals for food. They have keen eyesight, powerful hooked bills, and strong feet, each with four sharp, curved claws called talons.

- **Most birds of prey** seize their prey with their talons and use their bills to tear up their food.

- **The true falcons** kill their prey with their beaks. A toothlike ridge along the top part of the bills breaks the backbone of their prey.

- **Most birds of prey** sometimes feed on dead animals (carrion), and this is the main source of food for vultures.

- **In captivity**, birds of prey live for 50 years or more. One Andean condor is known to have lived for 72 years.

▼ *Tawny owls feed their chicks (called owlets) on mice and voles for up to three months.*

► The kestrel is one of the world's most common birds of prey. Males (right) have chestnut backs with gray heads and tails. Females are brown with dark bars on their backs and tails.

🦅 **Birds of prey** usually build large nests of twigs and branches. They tend to mate for life, using the same nest over many years.

🦅 **Birds of prey** lay few eggs and their young take up to six years, or even as long as ten years, to reach maturity.

🦅 **There are two main groups** of birds of prey: the raptors (such as hawks, eagles, vultures, and falcons), which are active during the day, and the owls, which are nocturnal. They look similar because they have similar lifestyles, but are probably not closely related.

🦅 **The word raptor** comes from the Latin word *rapere*, meaning "to seize or grasp," because these birds seize their prey in their feet.

🦅 **There are more than 300 species** of raptors and over 200 species of owls.

203

# Goshawks and sparrowhawks

- **Goshawks and sparrowhawks** feed mainly or entirely on other birds. They pluck the feathers off their prey before eating them, as they cannot digest the feathers.

- **Adult goshawks and sparrowhawks** soar over their breeding territory together, using long, slow wingbeats.

- **Young goshawks** first leave the nest at about 40 days old and start to fly at about 45 days. By 50 days or so they have learnt to hunt for themselves, and by 70 days they can manage without their parents.

- **Fledgling goshawks** "play" as a way of practising their hunting skills.

- **The largest hawk** is the northern goshawk, which is up to 23 in long and weighs as much as 46 lb.

◀ *The pale chanting goshawk is an African bird that often perches on open branches or walks on the ground. It lives in a dry, open, semi-desert habitat and feeds mainly on lizards.*

▲ The sparrowhawk preys mostly on other birds, ranging in size from tits to pheasants.

🦅 **Northern goshawks** are powerful birds. The females can catch prey as large as pheasants, wood pigeons, or hares.

🦅 **The dark chanting goshawk** is named after the whistling "chants" it makes from the tops of trees during the breeding season.

🦅 **Sparrowhawks** living in northern regions may migrate south to Africa or parts of southern Asia for the winter months.

🦅 **A sparrowhawk will sometimes hunt** like a peregrine, diving down onto its prey from a great height.

🦅 **The female sparrowhawk** is up to 25 percent larger than the male. At breeding time she defends the nest, while the more agile male brings the family food.

# Harriers and harrier hawks

▶ *The adult male hen harrier is pale gray above and white below, whereas the female is brown above with brown-and-white streaks below. The male is smaller than the female.*

- **Harriers are slender** birds of prey with long wings and long legs.

- **Harriers usually** nest on the ground, which is unusual for birds of prey.

- **The feathers** on a harrier's face are arranged to help funnel sound to their ears. This helps them to hear prey when they hunt in dense reeds or grasses.

- **Hen harriers** (also called northern harriers or marsh hawks) hunt by flying slowly above the ground, taking their prey, such as small rodents, by surprise. These hawks are the only harriers to live in North America.

- **Out of the breeding season**, hen harriers sometimes gather in roosts of ten to 20 birds. Up to 200 birds have sometimes been recorded roosting together.

**DID YOU KNOW?**

The word harrier comes from the Old English word "hergian," meaning to harass, ravage, or plunder.

🦇 **Female hen harriers** and marsh harriers fly up from the nest to catch food dropped by the male. They turn upside down and catch the food in mid-air with their feet.

🦇 **In their courtship flight**, marsh harriers fly high in the sky, diving and somersaulting down to the ground. The male often passes food to the female during these displays.

🦇 **The African harrier hawk** likes to feed on baby birds. It has long, double-jointed legs that allow it to reach into other birds' nests and grab the chicks.

🦇 **The crane hawk** of Central and South America usually lives near water. It often lives in woodlands with pools and streams, or swamp forests.

◄ When harriers, such as this marsh harrier, are gliding or soaring, they hold their wings in a shallow "V" shape.

207

# Buzzards and kites

- **One of the most common** of all birds of prey is the black kite, which lives throughout most of Europe, Africa, Asia, and Australia.

- **The black kite** is a scavenger as well as a hunter. It will take food from dustbins and even market stalls!

- **Hundreds of years ago**, red kites were commonly seen on the Tudor streets of London, England, where they scavenged from the city's rubbish heaps. Nowadays, it lives only in the countryside in the UK and is a rare bird.

- **The red kite** often takes over the old nest of a raven.

◀ The yellow legs of the Eurasian buzzard are not covered in feathers, which is one way of distinguishing it from the rough-legged buzzard, which looks similar.

◄ The graceful swallow-tailed kite spends most of the day floating effortlessly on air currents, sometimes swooping down to grab lizards and snakes from the ground.

**Kites have** distinctive forked tails. This shape works like a rudder, helping the kite to change direction quickly and allowing it to move around obstacles with ease.

**The American swallow-tailed kite** has a tail shaped like that of a real swallow. It often behaves in a similar way, catching flying insects and skimming the water's surface to drink and bathe.

**A buzzard** can spot a rabbit popping up out of its burrow from almost 2 mi away.

**The rough-legged buzzard** is common over open tundra in the far north. It preys on rodents and rabbits.

**In spring**, the Eurasian buzzard has a spectacular courtship display. Males and females pass sticks to each other in mid-air and sometimes lock their feet together as they tumble down to the ground.

**Jackal buzzards** often feed on carrion by the roadside in Africa, even flying between the cars.

209

# Snake and sea eagles

- **The bald eagle** performs an amazing courtship display, in which the male and female lock their claws together and tumble through the air to the ground.

- **Bald eagles** are not really bald. They have white feathers on their heads, which may make them appear bald from a distance.

- **The bald eagle** is able to catch a salmon that weighs as much as its own body weight.

- **In 1782** the bald eagle was chosen as the national emblem of the U.S., and it appears on most of the gold and silver coins in the U.S.

- **The white-tailed sea eagle** snatches fish from the water using its sharp, powerful talons.

- **Spikes** on the underside of its toes help the African fish eagle hold onto its fish prey. It also catches birds, terrapins, and baby crocodiles.

▲ The distinctive, adaptable bateleur eagle is widespread across Africa in grassland, mountain and desert regions.

- **Snake eagles** eat snakes and have short, strong toes ideal for tackling their writhing victims.

- **The short-toed eagle** kills a snake with a bite to the back of the head, instantly severing the backbone.

- **The bateleur**, a snake eagle, may fly almost 200 mi a day in search of food.

- **The word** *bateleur* means "tumbler" or "tightrope walker," so the bateleur eagle is named for the rocking, acrobatic movements that it makes in flight.

▼ The bald eagle catches a lot of fish, snatching them from the water with its lethally sharp talons.

211

# True and harpy eagles

🦅 **The golden eagle** makes a bulky nest of sticks and branches (an eyrie) that may measure as much as 6.6 ft high and 5 ft across.

🦅 **Golden eagles** usually have a hunting territory of about 100 sq mi.

▼ Golden eagles lay two eggs, but one of the chicks usually dies. At first the mother keeps the surviving chick warm while the male finds food, but as the chick grows larger, both parents are kept busy supplying it with food.

Hooked beak for tearing apart its prey

Large eyes— the eagle has excellent eyesight

Tapering wing feathers increase lift so the eagle can soar for long periods

Long curved talons

▶ *The harpy eagle flies through the treetops of the South American rain forests at speeds of up to 50 mph. It uses its powerful hooked beak to tear the flesh from its prey.*

- **The most powerful of all eagles,** the South American harpy eagle hunts prey that may weigh more than itself, such as large monkeys and sloths.

- **A harpy eagle** weighs over 17 lb, has a wingspan of more than 6.5 ft, and talons the size of a bear's claws.

- **The male crowned eagle** of Africa shows off its chestnut underwings to its mate during its courtship display.

- **True eagles** are also known as booted eagles, because their legs are covered with feathers down to their toes.

- **Verreaux's eagle** lays two eggs, but the first chick to hatch usually kills the younger chick.

- **At up to 38 in long**, the martial eagle is the largest African eagle. It feeds on mammals such as hyraxes and young antelope, and on other birds, including guineafowl and even storks.

- **A young martial eagle** is fed by its parents for about 60 days, by which time it has a full covering of feathers and is able to tear up prey for itself.

# Falcons and caracaras

- **The peregrine falcon's hunting** technique is so demanding that only one in ten attacks is successful.

- **At up to 24 in long**, the gyrfalcon is the largest species in the falcon family, and can catch ducks and hares.

- **The common kestrel** hovers above the ground on fast-beating wings while it searches for small mammals.

- **In winter**, both male and female kestrels spend about a quarter of their day hunting. But when the female is incubating eggs, the male hunts for longer.

- **Eleonora's falcon** is named after a 14th-century Sardinian princess, who brought in laws to protect it.

- **Falconets and pygmy falcons** are the smallest birds of prey. The Philippine falconet is only 6 in long.

▼ *Like other birds of prey, the gyrfalcon has exceptionally sharp eyesight, which helps it find prey.*

▲ Peregrines use their wings and body to "cloak" or hide their prey. A peregrine can eat a meal weighing as much as one quarter of its own weight in one sitting.

DID YOU KNOW?
Kestrels can see ultraviolet light, which reflects off the urine a rodent uses to mark its tracks.

**Caracaras** are chicken-sized birds of prey, related to falcons. They have long legs, with flat claws on their toes, and can move quickly to avoid danger. They often join vultures to feed on animal carcasses, but they also feed on a variety of live prey, such as birds, fish, frogs, small mammals, and insects.

**The yellow-headed caracara** sometimes perches on the backs of farm animals to feed on the ticks on their skin.

▶ The tiny black-thighed falconet is only 6.3 in long and is one of the smallest birds of prey. It flies out from a perch in the forests to catch insects and small birds.

215

# Ospreys and secretary birds

🦅 **Both the osprey and the secretary bird** have a family all to themselves, as no other birds are quite like them.

🦅 **The osprey** was described by Aristotle as early as 350 BC.

🦅 **When fishing**, the osprey plunges into the water feet first and grasps its slithery prey with its spine-covered feet.

🦅 **An osprey** usually has to make three or four dives into the water before it succeeds in catching a fish.

🦅 **Male ospreys** feed the whole family once the chicks have hatched.

◄ *The osprey's body measures 22–23 in long, and it has an impressive wingspan of 5.3 ft. The females are slightly larger than the males.*

▶ The secretary bird often kills snakes by stamping on them with its short, stubby toes.

🦊 **The secretary bird** is the tallest bird of prey. It stands up to 4 ft tall and its wingspan can reach over 6.5 ft.

🦊 **Secretary birds** pair up for life. They sleep side by side in their nest, which they live in all year round, not just in the breeding season.

🦊 **A secretary bird chick** grows all its feathers in five weeks, but stays in the nest for about a month longer.

🦊 **The long legs** of the secretary bird enable it to walk easily through the tall grasses on the African savanna.

🦊 **Secretary birds** are so-called because of the quill-like crests on the backs of their heads.

# New World vultures

🦅 **There are seven species of New World vultures** in North and South America. Like Old World vultures, their diet includes carrion, but they have weaker, thinner beaks than Old World vultures.

🦅 **New World vultures** do not build nests, but simply lay their eggs on the ground or on cliff ledges. The parent birds feed their young on regurgitated food.

🦅 **New World** vultures have weak feet, rather like those of chickens. They cannot lift and carry food with their feet, but they do step on their food to hold it in place.

▶ The Andean condor is 3.3 ft or more in length, with black-and-white plumage and distinctive wing feathers, which are splayed out like fingers during flight.

◀ *Unusually colorful for a bird of prey, the king vulture has bright red, orange, and yellow bare skin and wattles (loose folds of skin) on its head.*

- **The king vulture** has a particularly good sense of smell and can find carrion even in dense rain forests.

- **King vultures** have stronger beaks than other New World vultures and are able to tear apart large animals.

- **Pairs of turkey vultures** raise their young together. The female usually lays up to three eggs, and both parents help to incubate them for up to 41 days.

- **Black vulture chicks** are looked after by both parents. They do not fly until they are 11 weeks old.

- **Vultures** can go for weeks without food. When they do find carrion, they eat as much as possible.

- **The largest of all birds of prey** is the Andean condor, with a wingspan of more than 10 ft.

- **The Andean condor** soars high in the sky on outstretched wings, sometimes rising to heights of 23,000 ft over the mountains. It has very keen eyesight and can spot dead animals from great heights.

# Old World vultures

- **Most vultures are scavengers** rather than hunters—they feed on the carcasses of dead animals.

- **The lack of feathers** on a vulture's head means that it does not have to do lots of preening after it has plunged its beak deep into a carcass to feed.

- **Different species** of vulture eat different parts of a body—bearded vultures (lammergeiers) even eat the bones of their prey.

- **In hot weather**, some vultures cool down by squirting urine onto their legs.

- **There are about 15 species** of Old World vulture living in southern Europe, Africa, and Asia.

◀ *This Egyptian vulture is about to break open a thick-shelled ostrich egg with a stone so that it can eat the contents. Its hooked beak is perfect for pecking scraps of meat from bones.*

▲ The lappet-faced vulture has a bigger beak than any other bird of prey. Old World vultures generally have stronger beaks than New World vultures.

■ **Unlike most birds of prey,** the palm-nut vulture is mostly vegetarian. Its main food is the husk of the oil palm fruit, although it also eats fish, frogs, and other small creatures.

■ **The European black vulture** is the biggest of all the Old World vultures. It weighs up to 26.5 lb and has a wingspan of over 9 ft.

■ **The female white-backed vulture** lays one egg in a large stick nest made high in a tree. She incubates the egg for 56 days, being fed by the male. Both parents feed and care for the chick.

■ **The lappet-faced vulture** is the largest vulture in Africa—it measures about 3 ft long and has a huge 9.2 ft wingspan.

# Owls

- **The 150 or so species of owl** live in most parts of the world except the far north and Antarctica.

- **Owls range** in size from the least pygmy owl, at only 4.7–5.5 in long, to the Eurasian eagle owl, at 28 in long.

- **The soft, fluffy edges** of an owl's feathers help to reduce flight noise, so it can hunt almost silently.

- **The "disk" of feathers** on an owl's face helps to focus sounds, enabling it to hear the noises made by its prey in the dark.

- **The name** for a group of owls is a "parliament."

- **Female owls** are usually larger than males.

▼ Eagle owls are the largest owls in the world, able to overcome prey as large as small deer. They also prey on other owls.

▲ *When threatened, the fierce pygmy owl puffs up its feathers and spreads out its tail to make itself look larger. This tough little owl is able to carry prey three times its own weight.*

**Owls swallow their prey,** such as mice and insects, whole.

**Owls cannot digest** the bones, fur, and feathers of their prey, so they cough them up in the form of large pellets.

**Feathered legs and toes** help to protect owls from the bites of their prey.

**Some Native Americans** believed that owls were the souls of people and should never be harmed.

223

# Owl families

- **Owls are divided** into two main groups—the 18 species of barn owls, grass owls, and the bay owl, and the nearly 200 species of typical owls.

- **Barn owls, grass owls, and the bay owl** have a heart-shaped disk on their faces, rather than the round disk of typical owls.

- **They also** have a longer bill and legs and longer, more pointed wings than typical owls. Their tails are forked.

- **Grass owls** come from Africa, Southeast Asia, and Australia. They are very similar to barn owls but have longer legs.

- **Barn owls** lay between four and seven white eggs in tree holes or old buildings, but they do not make nests.

◀ The huge great grey owl has a wingspan of about 5 ft. It feeds largely on tiny voles. This owl defends its nest hole fiercely and will even attack people if it feels threatened.

▲ *A barn owl swoops silently down onto its unsuspecting prey, holding out its sharp talons to seize its meal.*

**Eagle owls** have a wingspan of about 6.6 ft and are twice the size of barn owls. They live for up to 40 years in the wild.

**The boobook owl** of Australia, New Zealand, and New Guinea is named after the sound of its high-pitched call.

**The hawk owl** is one of the few owls that are active during the daytime. It feeds on birds and small mammals, such as voles.

**The brown fish owl** has bare legs and feet—feathers would get clogged with fish scales.

**The little owl** is only 0.7 in long and feeds mainly on insects, such as beetles. It bobs its head up and down when it is agitated or anxious.

225

# Waders and water birds

# Waders or shorebirds

- **Waders are called shorebirds** in North America. They live near shallow water on coasts, lakes, meadows, marshes, and other wetlands all over the world.

- **The wader family** includes over 200 species, such as jacanas, avocets, oystercatchers, plovers, stilts, lapwings, sandpipers, and snipes.

- **Most waders** are small or medium-size birds with long, slender legs and long, sensitive bills.

- **A wader** often probes wet sand, mud, or grass to find small animals to eat. Each species of wader has a characteristic length and shape of bill according to the way it feeds.

▼ *South American wattled jacanas use their long bills to probe for snails, insects, and small fish among the tangled vegetation in ponds, marshes, streams, and flooded meadows.*

🦃 **Different bill lengths** allow different species of waders to feed close together because they each feed at different depths in the mud or water.

🦃 **Many waders** breed in the north of the world during the summer months and migrate long distances to warmer places in the south for the winter.

🦃 **Migrating flocks of waders** may contain tens of thousands of birds.

🦃 **Waders lay their eggs** on the ground and their chicks have fluffy feathers when they hatch.

🦃 **The biggest wader** is the curlew, which is about the size of a mallard, but has a longer, more slender shape.

▲ The black-tailed godwit is a long-legged wader of marshes, flooded fields, and estuaries. In summer, adults have chestnut heads, necks, and breasts, but their winter plumage is a dull gray color.

🦃 **The smallest waders** are the least sandpiper and the little stint, which are both about the size of sparrows.

229

# Sandpipers and snipes

- **Sandpipers** are the largest family of wading birds, with about 90 species.

- **The sandpiper and snipe family** also includes curlews, dowitchers, dunlins, godwits, redshanks, sanderlings, and turnstones.

- **During migration**, bar-tailed godwits sometimes fly for 6,000 mi without stopping to rest or feed.

- **Sandpipers incubate their eggs** for 18–30 days and the young are quite independent as soon as they hatch.

- **The western curlew** plunges its long, curved beak into soft coastal mud to find worms and clams.

- **As it dives toward Earth**, air rushing through the outermost tail feathers of the European snipe makes a sound called "drumming."

▼ *The purple sandpiper finds its prey by sight along the water's edge. It is named after the purple tinge on its upper feathers but its mottled plumage blends easily with a background of beach boulders.*

DID YOU KNO
Red knots travel up t
18,600 mi twice a yea.
as they migrate betwee
their breeding grounds
in Canada and their
wintering grounds in
South America.

◄ Red legs are the most obvious identifying feature of a redshank. If danger threatens, redshanks fly up into the air, making a series of harsh, piping alarm calls.

🐾 **Once the dowitcher's four eggs** have hatched, feeding the chicks is the sole responsibility of the male.

🐾 **Unusually for birds,** female phalaropes are more brightly colored than males. The female lays several clutches of eggs, leaving the male parent of each clutch to care for the young.

🐾 **The turnstone** is so-called because it turns over stones on the beach when searching for shellfish and worms.

🐾 **In the breeding season**, male ruffs grow amazing feathers around their heads and necks, and dance in groups to attract females.

◄ The curlew's long legs are ideal for wading over marshland.

231

# Plovers and lapwings

- **There are 60 or so species** of plovers and lapwings (also known as peewits) around the world.

- **The wrybill**, a New Zealand plover, has a unique beak that curves to the right. The bird sweeps its beak over sand to pick up insects.

- **The markings** of Kentish plover chicks look like the stones and pebbles of their nest site. If danger threatens, the chicks flatten themselves on the ground and are almost impossible to see.

- **Female dotterels** lay clutches of eggs for several males, which incubate the eggs.

- **To attract females**, the male lapwing performs a spectacular rolling, tumbling display flight.

- **Spur-winged plovers** are often seen close to crocodiles in Africa and Asia—they may feed on small creatures that the crocodiles disturb.

◀▼ *The ringed plover (left) breeds in the Canadian Arctic and spends the winter in Europe and Africa. The blacksmith plover (below) lives on the wetlands of Kenya and parts of southern Africa.*

▲ The lapwing is sometimes called the green plover, after the greenish, iridescent plumage on its back. When it flies, its white underparts are very obvious and its broad, rounded wings are different from those of other waders.

- **Most plovers** feed on insects, shellfish, and worms.

- **Golden plovers** have been recorded flying at speeds of more than 70 mph.

- **The blacksmith plover** is named after its harsh call, which sounds like a blacksmith striking an anvil with a hammer.

**DID YOU KNOW?**

Many plovers pat the ground with their feet to imitate the sound of rain. This draws worms to the surface, where they are snapped up.

233

# Oystercatchers and relatives

- **The oystercatcher** uses its strong, bladelike beak to prise mussels off rocks and open their shells.

- **Oystercatcher chicks** stay with their parents for up to one year while they learn how to find and open shellfish.

- **The 17 species** in the courser and pratincole family live in southern Europe, Asia, Africa, and Australia.

- **The Egyptian plover** (courser family) buries its eggs in sand and leaves them to be incubated by the warmth of the sun. The parents sit on the eggs at night, and if the weather is cool.

- **If the Egyptian plover's** chicks get too hot, the parent birds soak their own belly feathers with water and give their young a cooling shower.

▶ *The common pratincole feeds on insects and will follow swarms of locusts.*

▶ The common oystercatcher breeds in Europe and Asia, but spends the winter in South Africa and southern Asia.

**The cream-colored courser** has pale, sandy feathers that help to keep it hidden in its desert home.

**The common pratincole** nests on sand or rocks, and lays two to four mottled, well-camouflaged eggs. The parents take turns to incubate the eggs for 17–18 days.

**The nine species** in the thick-knee family include the stone curlew and the dikkop. These long-legged birds usually feed at night on insects, worms, and shellfish.

**The thick-knees** get their common name from the knobbly joints on their legs—actually between the ankle and shin bones.

**The pygmy seed-snipe** of southern South America blends in with the plains landscape so well that it is almost invisible when it crouches on the ground.

235

# Avocets and relatives

▲ The jacana is sometimes called the "lily-trotter" because of its unique way of moving over the leaves of water plants.

- **The seven species of stilts** and avocets are all long-legged wading birds with long, slender beaks.

- **Avocets lay about four eggs** in a hollow in open ground. The female avocet spreads her wings to shelter her eggs from the sun.

- **Avocets nest in a hollow** in the ground, lined with dead leaves. Both partners incubate the three to five eggs.

- **Young avocets** can run soon after hatching, and can fend for themselves after six weeks.

- **Jacanas** range in size from 6–21 in long.

- **Female pheasant-tailed jacanas** mate with up to ten males in one breeding season. The males incubate the eggs and care for the young.

DID YOU KNOW?
Jacanas have extremely long toes and claws that spread their weight, allowing them to walk on floating water-lily leaves.

- **If a male pheasant-tailed jacana** thinks its eggs are in danger, it may move them one at a time, holding them between its breast and throat.

- **Northern jacanas** are quarrelsome birds. They often fight each other using the sharp spurs on their wings as weapons.

- **The black-winged stilt** has extremely long, bright-pink legs that allow it to wade in deeper water than other stilts as it searches for worms and shellfish.

▼ The long, curved beak of the pied avocet turns up at the end. The bird sweeps this strange tool through mud or shallow water to find worms and shrimps.

# Penguins

- **Not all of the 18 species** of penguin live in Antarctica. A few species live around Australia and South Africa, and there is even one resident in the Galápagos Islands on the Equator.

- **Penguins have wings**, but cannot fly. They spend as much as 85 percent of their time in water, where they use their wings like flippers to help push themselves through the water.

- **The king penguin** has been known to dive down to 820 ft in search of prey.

- **An emperor penguin** may travel at least 560 mi on a single feeding expedition.

- **Like many other penguins**, gentoos nest in a simple hollow in the ground, but they surround it with a ring of pebbles. A courting gentoo shows its mate an example of the sort of pebbles it will provide.

▶ A chinstrap penguin chick waits for its parent to regurgitate (cough up) a meal of fishy food from its stomach. Penguin chicks grow fast and are always hungry.

▶ A king penguin incubates its egg by holding it on its feet against a bare, warm patch of skin called a brood patch. Both parents take it in turns to keep their egg warm.

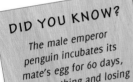

DID YOU KNOW?

The male emperor penguin incubates its mate's egg for 60 days, eating nothing and losing as much as 45 percent of his body weight.

- **The emperor penguin** keeps its egg warm on its feet, where it is covered by a fold of skin. The temperature there stays at a constant 96.8°C, despite the freezing surroundings.

- **Penguins** eat fish, squid, and shellfish. They have spiny tongues to help them hold on to slippery prey.

- **An extremely dense covering** of three layers of feathers keeps penguins warm.

- **Penguins** usually swim at 3–6 mph, but can reach speeds of up to 15 mph.

# Auks

- **The auk family** includes 22 species of diving birds, including auks, guillemots, puffins, and razorbills. They live in and around the North Pacific, Atlantic, and Arctic Oceans.

- **The common guillemot** is the largest of the auks, at about 18 in long and 2.2 lb in weight. The least auklet is the smallest auk, at 6.3 in long and 3.2 oz.

- **Common guillemots** nest in colonies of thousands.

- **The common guillemot nests** on narrow cliff ledges. Its eggs are pointed, so that if they get knocked, they roll in a circle and do not fall off.

- **The ancient murrelet** is so-called because it develops fine white feathers on its head in the breeding season. These are said to look like the white hairs of an elderly person.

- **The guillemot** can dive to a depth of 330 ft as it hunts.

▲ Guillemots have dagger-shaped bills for seizing fish when diving. Their streamlined shape helps them to move through water, and they use their webbed feet for steering.

**DID YOU KNOW?**
The puffin flies at up to 55 mph, with its wings beating 300–400 times a minute.

- **The little auk** nests in cliff crevices and lays one or two eggs, which both parents incubate.

- **The razorbill** is named after its very sharp bill, which helps it to hold slippery fish and other sea creatures, as well as being a useful means of defense against predators.

- **Razorbill chicks** are only 10–18 days old when they flutter down to the sea from their nests on the cliffs.

▶ The red, yellow, and blue bill of the puffin fades after the breeding season when the colorful outer scales are shed.

# Divers and grebes

- **Divers feed only on fish**, which they catch underwater. The great northern diver can dive to depths of 65 ft or more.

- **Divers are so well-adapted** for diving and swimming that adult birds cannot walk upright on land.

- **At 3 ft long**, the white-billed diver is the largest of the four species of diver.

- **The chicks** of great northern divers leave the nest a day or so after hatching. They spend the next two or three months with their parents, often riding on their backs to keep warm.

▼ The red-necked grebe builds a floating nest of water plants, anchored to other vegetation. Most of the nest is below the water. The female lays four or five eggs, which both parents incubate.

**DID YOU KNOW?**
Grebes have up to 20,000 feathers to keep their bodies warm and dry as they dive for food.

◄ *The great crested grebe lives in parts of Europe, Asia, Africa, and Australasia.*

There are about 20 species of grebe, three of them flightless. They live near freshwater lakes and marshes.

Grebes feed on fish, insects, and shellfish. They swallow molted feathers, which may help them regurgitate waste such as fish bones and keep their guts free of parasites.

The short-winged grebe lives on lakes high in the mountains of Peru and Bolivia, and cannot fly. It basks in the sun to warm its body up after a cold night.

The great crested grebe makes a nest of water plants floating near the water's edge. It lays three to six eggs, which both male and female incubate.

Little grebes chase rivals away from their territories, rushing low over the water while splashing, diving, and calling loudly.

243

# Albatrosses

▶ Squid is the main food of the wandering albatross, but it will also snatch fish waste thrown from fishing boats. An expert glider, it can sail downwind from a height of about 50 ft to just above the water's surface, before turning back into the wind to be blown upward.

**DID YOU KNOW?**

Wandering albatross chicks sit on the nest for nearly ten months, which makes them nearly a year old before they are ready to fly.

🦆 **There are 14 species of albatross**, including the royal, wandering, waved, Laysan, sooty, black-browed and gray-headed albatrosses. These large birds have a body length of between 33 and 53 in.

🦆 **Albatrosses** spend nearly 90 percent of their lives over the oceans, coming to land only to nest and raise their chicks.

🦆 **The wandering albatross** has the longest wings of any bird— from tip to tip they are an incredible 11 ft.

🦆 **The wandering albatross** often flies hundreds of miles in a day, soaring over the ocean in search of food.

- **The wandering albatross** can only breed every other year, and incubates its eggs for 11 weeks.

- **Wandering albatrosses** have 88 flight feathers, which is more than any other bird.

- **On their extra-long wings**, wandering albatrosses glide at speeds of almost 56 mph. They are such efficient gliders that they rarely need to flap their wings.

- **Sooty albatrosses** breed on steep cliffs or near slopes, which help them to take off easily.

- **Pairs of waved albatrosses** take part in a complex courtship dance, during which they make loud "ha-ha" noises.

▶ Named after its characteristic black "eyebrow," the black-browed albatross usually mates for life. Parents rear one chick a year, which stays on the nest for about four months and is fed by both parents.

245

# Shearwaters and petrels

🦆 **The 70 or more species** in the shearwater family include petrels, fulmars, and prions. They range from the Antarctic to the Arctic.

🦆 **Unlike most birds,** shearwaters and petrels have a good sense of smell. They have long, tube-shaped nostrils on the tops of their beaks.

🦆 **Shearwaters and petrels** are not tuneful birds, and at night the colonies make a very loud, harsh noise.

🦆 **Shearwaters' legs** are placed far back on their bodies, making them expert swimmers, but preventing them from standing up properly. They move awkwardly on land and have to launch themselves into the air from trees.

◄ Storm petrels often patter their feet over the water's surface when hunting for fish.

- **Largest of the shearwater family** are the giant petrels. At 3 ft long, they are bigger than some albatrosses.

- **Fish and squid** are the main food of shearwaters, but giant petrels also feed on carrion, and can rip apart whales and seals with their powerful beaks.

- **The manx shearwater** lays one egg in a burrow. The male and female take turns incubating it and feeding one another.

- **Young shearwaters** are fed on a rich mixture of regurgitated fish and squid, and may put on weight so quickly that they are soon heavier than their parents.

- **Prions feed on tiny plankton**, which they filter from the water through comblike structures at the sides of their beaks.

▼ Manx shearwaters nest in colonies of thousands of birds on offshore islands or isolated cliff tops.

**DID YOU KNOW?**
To defend themselves, shearwaters can spit out food and fish oil to a distance of 3 ft.

247

# Gannets and boobies

- **There are three species of gannet** and six species of booby. Boobies generally live in tropical and subtropical areas, while gannets live in cooler, temperate parts of the world.

- **The gannet** plunges 330 ft or so through the air and dives into the water to catch prey such as herring and mackerel.

- **A specially strengthened skull** helps cushion the impact of the gannet's high-speed dive into water.

- **Gannets usually** lay just one egg, which both parents help to incubate for 43–45 days. They feed their chick with regurgitated food for up to 13 weeks.

- **When one gannet parent** arrives at the nest to take over incubating the egg, it presents its mate with a piece of seaweed, which is then added to the nest.

▶ Cape gannets reinforce their pair bond by "fencing" with their bills. Both birds then help each other to build a nest and defend their territory.

▲ *The downy chicks of blue-footed boobies take nearly four months to grow their adult feathers and are dependent on their parents for food and protection for another two months after this.*

**Young gannets** and boobies are kept warm on their mother's feet for their first few weeks.

**Boobies** were given their common name because they were so easy for sailors to catch and kill.

**The male blue-footed booby** attracts a mate by dancing and holding up its brightly colored feet as it struts about.

**Boobies** spend the majority of their time at sea, only landing to breed and rear their young.

**At up to 2.8 ft long** and with a wingspan of 5 ft, the masked booby is the largest of the boobies.

# Terns and skimmers

- **The 42 or so species of terns** are found all over the world, mostly along coasts.

- **The noddy**, a species of tern, gets its name from its habit of nodding its head during its courtship display.

- **The black skimmer's beak** has a flattened lower part that is longer than the upper part. The bird flies over water with the lower part of its beak just below the surface, ready to snap up prey.

- **Arctic terns** are long-lived birds, known to survive to 27—and sometimes even 34—years of age.

- **Most terns** eat fish, squid, and shellfish, but marshland terns also eat insects and frogs.

▼ Skimmers are so-called because of the way they "skim" the water for fish with their sensitive beaks.

▼ The Arctic tern has a long, forked tail, short red legs, a pointed beak, and a covering of black feathers on its head.

**DID YOU KNOW?**

Over a lifetime of migration journeys, an Arctic tern travels the equivalent distance of three trips to the Moon and back.

- **At up to 2 ft long**, the Caspian tern is the largest of the terns, and one of the most widespread.

- **The fairy tern** does not make a nest. Instead, it balances its one egg on a tree branch and manages to sit on it without knocking it off.

- **Most terns** mate for life. Even if they don't stay together all year round, pairs meet up when they return to breeding sites.

- **There are only three species** of skimmers. All live in areas of tropical Africa, Southeast Asia, and North and South America.

# Gulls and relatives

- **There are about 50 species** of gull found on shores and islands all over the world.

- **The great skua** is a pirate—it chases other birds and forces them to give up their prey in midair.

- **The snowy sheathbill** scavenges for food on Antarctic research bases, and also steals eggs and chicks from penguin colonies.

- **Arctic glaucous and ivory gulls** sometimes feed on the feces of marine mammals.

▲ Skuas are found in marine habitats close to Antarctica and the Arctic.

▼ Black wingtips with white spots or patches help to identify a herring gull. Chicks peck at the red spot on the bill to stimulate their parents to regurgitate (cough up) food.

- **At up to 2.5 ft long**, the great black-backed gull is the giant of the group. The little gull is one of the smallest, at 11 in long.

- **The Arctic explorer** James Clark Ross discovered Ross's gull in the 19th century.

- **Skuas, also called jaegers**, usually lay two eggs in a shallow, moss-lined nest on the ground. Both parents incubate the eggs and feed the young, which can fend for themselves after about seven weeks.

- **The kittiwake** spends much more time at sea than other gulls, and usually only comes to land in the breeding season. It has very short legs and rarely walks.

- **Herring gulls** have learned that they can find food in seaside towns, and many now nest on roofs instead of cliff ledges.

- **The south polar skua** lays two eggs, but the first chick to hatch usually kills the second.

▼ The kittiwake builds a nest of seaweed lined with grass. Both parents sit on the nest for about four weeks to incubate the eggs.

# Pelicans

- **The great white pelican** catches about 2.6 lb of fish a day in its large throat pouch.

- **The brown pelican** dives from a height of 50 ft above the water to catch fish below the surface.

- **There are seven species** of pelican. Most live and feed around fresh water, but the brown pelican is a coastal seabird.

- **One of the largest pelicans** is the Australian pelican, which is up to 6 ft long and weighs about 33 lb.

- **The white pelican** lays one or two eggs in a nest mound on the ground. Both parents incubate the eggs and care for the young.

- **Pelican chicks** are able to stand at three weeks old and can fly at 10–12 weeks old.

▲ The brown pelican spreads out its wings so they act like brakes to slow it down as it comes in to land on the water.

▲ Pelicans are often found in large colonies, particularly during the breeding season.

- **White pelicans** work as a group to herd fish into a shoal by swimming around them in a horseshoe formation. Then they scoop up pouchfuls of fish with their large beaks.

- **In flight**, a pelican flaps its wings 1.3 times a second. This is one of the slowest wingbeat speeds of any bird.

- **All four of a pelican's toes** are joined together by a web of skin, which helps the birds to paddle along when swimming.

- **There are two main groups** of pelicans: white pelicans, which nest on the ground, and gray or brown pelicans, which nest in trees. The Peruvian pelican nests on rocks by the sea.

# Cormorants and relatives

- **The pirates of the bird world** are frigatebirds, which often chase other seabirds in the air and harass them into giving up their catches.

- **Frigatebird chicks** depend on their parents for longer than most birds. They start to fly at about six months, but continue to be fed until they are one year old.

- **The four species of anhinga**, or darter, all live in freshwater in tropical parts of the world. They are all expert underwater hunters.

- **The feathers of cormorants** and darters lack waterproofing and quickly get soaked through. This makes the birds heavier in water and better able to dive for fish.

- **Cormorants migrate** in large, V-shaped flocks, like migrating geese.

**DID YOU KNOW?**
Some shags dive to an incredible depth of 380 ft to hunt for fish.

◄ *After diving for food, cormorants stand on rocks with their wings outstretched to dry.*

- **In parts of Asia**, fishermen use cormorants to catch fish—the birds dive for the fish but do not swallow them.

- **The biggest species of cormorant**, the great cormorant, is up to 3 ft long.

- **A great cormorant** eats about 15 percent of its body weight in fish a day. That's like an adult human eating more than 80 hamburgers a day.

- **The American darter**, or snake bird, swims with its neck held in a snakelike curve above the water's surface.

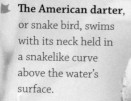

▶ *The male frigatebird has a bright red throat pouch that he inflates during courtship to attract females.*

257

# Herons and bitterns

- **There are about 60 species** of heron and bittern.

- **The great blue heron** makes a platform nest of twigs, often high in a tree. The four eggs take 25–29 days to hatch.

- **Like most herons**, the grey heron feeds on fish and frogs, which it catches with swift stabs of its beak.

- **When hunting,** the black heron holds its wings over its head like a sunshade. This may help the bird spot fish, or the patch of shade may attract fish to the area.

**DID YOU KNOW?**
The green-backed heron of Japan tempts fish with bits of "bait" such as bread or feathers.

◀ Herons are efficient hunters, using their long, sharp beaks to stab at fish.

▲ *The great egret catches fish and shellfish in shallow waters.*

- **Purple herons** have extra-long toes, which help them to walk over floating plants without sinking into the water.

- **The loud booming call** made by the male bittern in the breeding season can be heard up to 3.1 mi away.

- **The brown mottled plumage** of bitterns blends in with the reeds in the marshes where they live. When threatened, bitterns often point their bills to the sky and even sway to and fro like reeds in the wind.

- **Cattle egrets** nest in colonies—there may be more than 100 nests close together in one tree.

- **Cattle egrets** often gather around large grazing animals to feed on the insects and other small animals disturbed by their feet.

259

# Storks

- **The 19 species of stork** live in North and South America, Europe, Africa, Asia, and Australia.

- **In tropical areas**, storks' nests perched high on buildings can get very warm, so parents cool their young by regurgitating a shower of water over them.

- **The white stork** has long been a symbol of fertility in Europe. Parents used to tell their children that new babies were brought by a stork.

- **Marabou storks** often scavenge on rubbish tips.

- **The tail feathers of marabou storks** were once used to trim hats and dresses.

- **The upper and lower parts** of the openbill stork's beak meet only at the tip. This helps it to hold its favorite food of large snails.

◀ White storks build huge, bulky nests of branches and sticks, which may be up to 10 ft deep. Parent birds add to the nest each year, with the male bringing most of the extra materials.

- **When the wood stork's** partly open beak touches a fish under water, it snaps shut in 25 milliseconds—this is one of the fastest reactions of any animal.

- **Male and female white storks** take turns to incubate their clutch of three to five eggs. When the partners change shifts, they perform a special bill-clattering display.

- **The adjutant stork** is named after the adjutant army officer, because of its stiff, military-style walk.

- **The rooftop nests** of some European white storks have been used continuously for hundreds of years.

▼ Storks have long, spindly legs, plump bodies, and long bills for catching fish.

# Ibises and relatives

- **The spoonbill's beak** has a spoon-shaped tip that it uses to search shallow water for fish and small creatures.

- **At 4.6 ft in height** and weighing about 9 lb, the greater flamingo is the largest of the five species of flamingo.

- **The greater flamingo** has a wingspan of 4.5–5.3 ft.

- **The flamingo** feeds by forcing mud and water through bristly plates at each side of its beak with its tongue. Tiny creatures, algae, and other food particles are trapped and swallowed.

- **Until their beaks have developed fully,** young flamingos feed on a milky substance from their parents' throats.

▶ The scarlet ibis is one of the most striking birds in the world with its deep red plumage and black tail feathers.

Beak for filtering food from water

▶ The greater flamingo lives in huge flocks around lakes and deltas in Europe, Asia, parts of Africa, the Caribbean, and Central America. It may live to be at least 50 years old.

Long neck allows the bird to feed in deep water

🪶 **The glossy ibis** makes its nest in a reedbed or tree, and lays three or four eggs. The female does most of the incubation, but the male helps to rear the young.

🪶 **Young flamingos** have gray feathers at first. Adult birds get their pink color from pigments in the algae that they eat.

🪶 **Flamingos sleep** standing on one leg, with the other leg folded up and tucked underneath the body and the head laid over the back.

🪶 **When young flamingos** are able to walk around, they gather into small flocks, or crèches, which the adults take turns to guard from predators.

DID YOU KNOW?
Ibises and spoonbills are an ancient group of birds—fossils of their ancestors have been found that date back 60 million years.

# Dabbling ducks and relatives

- **There are more than 100 duck species.** They live all over the world, except Antarctica.

- **Most ducks** are good at flying. They take off almost vertically when alarmed and fly off with fast-beating wings.

- **Most common shelducks** nest in holes, such as old rabbit burrows in sand dunes or in hollow trees. The parents lead their ducklings to water.

- **Teal are typical "dabbling" ducks**, nibbling food (such as plant seeds or insects) from the surface of the water while swimming, or walking in shallow water.

- **In deeper water**, dabbling ducks often "upend" to reach food beneath the surface.

- **Wigeon are unusual ducks** because they often graze on grass, like geese.

- **The male garganey** throws back its head during its courtship display, which is a unique behavior for dabbling ducks.

◀ In the breeding season, the male teal has a chestnut head with a green eye patch. In flight, the black and yellow feathers under the tail show up well.

- **Male mallards** are usually more colorful than the females but they look very similar to the females when they molt their feathers.

- **Shovelers** are named after their rounded, shovel-like bills, which they use to strain tiny plants and animals from the surface of the water.

▲ *The male mandarin duck shows off his elaborate, colorful plumage in special courtship displays.*

- **In his breeding plumage**, the male pintail has a chocolate brown head, a gray-and-white body and a long, pointed tail. The female has dull, brown colors for camouflage on the nest.

▼ *A male ruddy shelduck can be distinguished from the female by the black ring at the base of its neck in the breeding season.*

▼ *The male shelduck has a knob at the base of his bill, which is missing in the female.*

265

# Diving ducks and relatives

- **Diving ducks**, such as pochard, scaup, and tufted ducks, dive underwater to collect food, such as shellfish, water plants, and insects.

- **Tufted ducks** dive down to depths of up to 20 ft and can stay underwater for up to 30 seconds.

- **Female scaup** lead their ducklings to water almost as soon as their downy feathers dry after hatching out. The chicks become independent when they are six weeks old.

- **The goldeneye** nests in tree holes and the chicks often tumble a long distance down to the ground when they leave the nest. They take eight weeks to grow their flight feathers.

- **The courtship display** of the male long-tailed duck includes a far-carrying yodeling call that sounds rather like someone playing the bagpipes.

▶ Barrow's goldeneye is a chunky diving duck named after John Barrow (a British Arctic explorer) and the golden color of its eyes. The male (shown here) has a crescent-shaped white patch at the base of the bill.

▲ *Long-tailed ducks have an unusual flying style, with shallow upstrokes but deep downstrokes of their wings. They are named for the long tail feathers of the male.*

**The male musk duck** has a pouch of skin under his bill, which produces a musky scent during the breeding season. The male is almost a third larger than the female.

**The female eider duck** lines her nest with soft down feathers that she pulls from her breast. Humans use the feathers too, to make quilts and sleeping bags.

**Like cuckoos**, the black-headed duck lays its eggs in the nests of other birds, such as coots. Just one day after hatching, the ducklings leave the nest to fend for themselves.

**The red-breasted merganser** is one of the fastest-flying birds. It can reach speeds of more than 40 mph—and possibly even 60 mph.

267

# Geese

- **Geese** feed mostly on leaves, and can eat as many as 100 blades of grass in one minute.

- **Snow geese** breed in the Arctic tundra, but fly south to spend the winter months around the Gulf of Mexico—a journey of some 3,000 mi.

- **In the winter**, snow geese gather in huge flocks that may contain tens of thousands of birds.

- **Red-breasted geese** often make their nests near those of peregrines and buzzards. This gives them protection, and they do not seem to get attacked by the birds of prey.

▼ *The greylag goose is a large goose with a wingspan of up to 5.5 ft.*

◀ The red-breasted goose breeds on the Arctic tundra of Russia but migrates mainly to Bulgaria and Romania for the winter months. This rare goose is threatened by hunting, industrial development, and the loss of its tundra habitat due to climate change.

## DID YOU KNOW?

Most birds fly at altitudes of up to 2,950 ft, but bar-headed geese are able to fly over the Himalayas at altitudes of up to 29,500 ft!

🦆 **Brant geese** are marine geese. They have special salt glands to help them drink saltwater and feed on salty eel grass, shellfish, and marine worms.

🦆 **Canada geese** can live for up to 30 years in the wild and even longer in captivity.

🦆 **The male magpie goose** has a high, bony crest on the top of his head, which helps him attract females.

🦆 **The toes** of the magpie goose are only partly webbed, so it is good at perching in trees.

🦆 **During their courtship display**, pairs of barnacle geese flick their wings and rush about, calling loudly.

# Swans

- **Whooper, trumpeter, and mute swans** are among the heaviest flying birds, weighing up to 35 lb.

- **The black swan** makes a nest of sticks and other plant material in shallow water and lays up to six eggs. Both parents help to incubate the eggs.

- **Tundra swans mate for life**, returning year after year to the same nesting site. They usually make their nests on marshland and lay three to five eggs.

- **Although quieter than other swans**, the mute swan is not really mute, as it makes many snorting and hissing calls.

▼ *A female mute swan swims with three of her cygnets. The cygnets are able to fly about eight weeks after hatching.*

◄ An adult whooper swan has a triangular-shaped head, with a large yellow patch on the bill.

🦢 **The swishing sound** of whooper and Bewick's swans in flight is quieter than that of mute swans, which make a loud twanging buzz as they fly.

🦢 **Whooper swans** are named after their loud trumpeting calls.

🦢 **Bewick's swans** have a smaller, rounder yellow patch on the bill than whooper swans.

🦢 **Each individual Bewick's or whooper swan** can be identified from its own unique bill pattern.

🦢 **It takes mute swan cygnets** nearly a year to grow their beautiful white feathers.

🦢 **Male swans** are known as "cobs," females as "pens," and baby swans are called "cygnets."

# Rails and relatives

- **There are more than 130 species** of rails found all over the world, including on many small islands. The family includes moorhens, coots, and crakes, as well as rails.

- **The takahe**, a large flightless rail, is now extremely rare and lives only in South Island, New Zealand.

- **Fights between Asian watercocks** (a type of rail) are staged for sport in some parts of Asia.

- **Coots are the most aquatic** of all rail species. They dive in search of plants and water insects to eat.

- **Female coots** often lay their eggs in their neighbor's nests as well as their own.

◀ *The American purple gallinule lives in freshwater marshes, using its long toes to help it walk over the lily pads. This bird has a colorful face, with a red-and-yellow bill, and a blue frontal shield.*

- **The female moorhen** makes a nest of dead leaves at the water's edge. The male helps incubate the five to 11 eggs.

- **Moorhen chicks** leave the nest when they are only two or three days old. They can already swim well at this very young age.

- **The water rail** makes loud groans and often sounds like a grunting or squealing pig.

- **The water rail's narrow body** helps it to slip soundlessly through reeds and other waterside plants in its swamp and marshland habitat.

- **Purple swamphens** often climb up the marshland vegetation to soak up the early morning rays of the sun.

▼ *The moorhen's nest is a platform of dried water plants, usually built among vegetation at the water's edge. The chicks become independent very quickly.*

# Finfoots and relatives

- **The sunbittern** gets its name from the rich, red-orange markings on its wings, which look like the colors of the sky at sunset.

- **The sungrebe** (finfoot family) has an unusual way of caring for its young. The male bird carries its chicks in two skin pouches beneath its wings while they complete their development. It can even carry them while flying.

- **The only species in its family**, the sunbittern lives in jungles and swamps in Central and South America.

- **The sunbittern** lays two eggs in a tree nest made of leaves and plant stems. Both parents take turns to incubate the eggs and care for the chicks.

▶ Finfoots lay two to seven eggs in a nest made among reeds or near water.

▲ *A sunbittern spreads its wings, showing off its beautiful plumage.*

- **Finfoots are aquatic birds** that feed in the water on fish, frogs, and shellfish. There is one species each in Africa, Southeast Asia, and Central and South America.

- **The two species of seriema** live in South America. They eat snakes, banging the snakes' heads on the ground to kill them.

- **Seriemas can fly,** but prefer to escape danger by running fast over the grassy plains where they live.

- **Sungrebes and finfoots** have lobed feet, which help them swim.

- **The rare kagu** lives only in the forests and shrubland of the Pacific island of New Caledonia. It has structures covering its nostrils, which are not found in any other bird.

- **The kagu** is almost flightless, but can use its wings to glide away from danger or move quickly through the forest. It also uses its wings for display.

# Game and ground birds

# Gamebirds

- **There are about 280 species** of gamebird, including turkeys, junglefowl, partridges, pheasants, grouse, and ptarmigans.

- **The name "gamebirds"** means that this group of birds were hunted for food or sport. Some are still hunted today, but many are domesticated and raised on farms.

- **Gamebirds** have plump bodies, small heads, and short legs. Most have powerful flight muscles and can fly for short distances.

- **The size of gamebirds** varies from tiny quails only 5.5 in long, to male peacocks, which reach lengths of up to 6.6 ft.

- **The short, thick bills** of gamebirds are adapted for eating seeds, insects, and grubs. They often use their feet to scratch for food.

- **Most gamebirds** feed on the ground and they often live and feed in large groups.

- **Male and female gamebirds** often look different. The female tends to be small and dull-colored for camouflage on the nest. The larger male often has brightly colored feathers for display.

DID YOU KNOW?

In spring, male turkeys make a "gobbling" sound to attract females. The "gobbling" can carry for up to one mile.

- **Most gamebirds** nest on the ground and lay large numbers of eggs.

- **Megapodes** are an unusual family of gamebirds because they do not incubate their eggs themselves. Instead they rely on the heat of rotting plants to keep their eggs warm.

**A male peacock** sheds its fabulous tail feathers every year and grows new ones ready for the next breeding season.

▼ *Wild turkeys are the heaviest gamebirds. Males (below) are larger than females and have iridescent feathers in shades of purple, green, and bronze.*

# Partridges and relatives

- **The partridge family** includes more than 90 species of partridges and francolins. They feed mainly on seeds.

- **In parts of Europe and North America**, partridges are reared in captivity and then released and shot for sport.

- **A group of partridges** is called a "covey." A covey usually contains a family of male, female, and young, plus a few other birds.

- **The long-billed wood partridge** lives at altitudes of up to 3,900 ft in the upland forests of Asia, particularly in areas of bamboo forest.

- **The female red-legged partridge** lays one clutch of eggs for her mate to incubate, and another to incubate herself.

- **The common quail** spends the winter in Africa, but migrates to Europe and parts of western Asia to breed in the summer months.

- **Tiny quail chicks** are born with their eyes open and their bodies covered in warm, downy feathers. They are able to follow their mother within one hour of hatching.

- **A mother quail** helps its chicks learn how to find food by pointing at food items with its beak.

- **At about 20 in long**, the vulturine guinea fowl is the largest of the six species of guinea fowl. It lives in Africa and eats fallen fruit.

- **Francolins** are large, powerful gamebirds of Africa and Asia, which have patches of bare skin on their heads or necks.

► The crested wood partridge (*1*) lives in the tropical rain forests of Southeast Asia. The male has a red, brushlike crest on his head. The Barbary partridge (*2*) lives in dry, open, often hilly country in North Africa, Gibraltar, and the Canary Islands. The Chinese painted quail (*3*) is the smallest of all the quails, reaching an average length of only 5.1 in. The male (shown here) is more colorful than the female.

# Pheasants and relatives

- **All 49 species of wild pheasant** are from Asia, except the Congo peafowl, which lives in the rain forests of central Africa.

- **To attract females**, the male great argus pheasant dances and spreads out its enormously long wing feathers.

- **The male great argus pheasant** plays no part in building a nest or raising the young.

- **The peacock's** wonderful train contains about 200 shimmering feathers, each one decorated with eyelike markings. When courting, the peacock spreads its train and makes it "shiver" to attract a female.

▶ *The peafowl is a native of India, Sri Lanka, and Pakistan, but it has been introduced in many areas throughout the world. Only the male (the peacock) has the spectacular tail, which does not reach its full glory until the bird is about three years old. It may continue to grow for another two to three years.*

- **The male pheasant** mates with several females, each of which lays up to 15 eggs in a shallow scrape on the ground. The females incubate the eggs for 23–27 days and the chicks are covered with downy feathers when they hatch out.

- **Most pheasants** nest on the ground, but the five species of tragopan, which live in tropical forests in Asia, nest in trees. They often take over the abandoned nests of other birds.

- **The satyr tragopan** lives high up on Asian mountains in the summer, but moves down to the lower slopes in winter.

- **The common pheasant** comes from Asia, but is now common in Australia, North America, and Europe, where it is shot for sport.

- **Male pheasants** have folds of red skin called wattles, hanging from the sides of their faces. The bright color helps them attract females.

- **In the breeding season**, male Himalayan snowcocks make whistling calls to impress females.

▶ The male common pheasant has iridescent plumage on its head, bright red wattles, and may have a white neck ring. Originally from Asia, this pheasant has been introduced in Europe and North America, where it is very common.

283

# Turkeys and grouse

- **Male wild turkeys** of the U.S., Mexico, and Central America can weigh up to 17.5 lb.

- **An adult turkey** has approximately 3,500 feathers.

- **Wild turkeys** are not fussy eaters. They feed on a variety of seeds, nuts, berries, leaves, insects, and other small creatures.

- **The 17 species of grouse** live in North America, Europe, and northern Asia.

- **At 34 in long**, the western capercaillie is the biggest of the 17 species of grouse.

◄ During the breeding season, male turkeys attract females by strutting about, fanning out their tails, and showing off their brightly colored throat wattles. The female turkeys (hens) look after the eggs and chicks on their own.

- **In winter,** the spruce grouse feeds mainly on the buds and needles of pine trees.

- **To attract females** and challenge rival males, the ruffed grouse makes a drumming sound with its wings.

- **The ruffed grouse lays nine to 12 eggs.** When the young hatch, the female shows them where to find food.

- **At the start of the breeding season,** foot-stamping dances are performed by groups of male prairie chickens at their traditional display areas.

▲ The dull plumage of the female spruce grouse helps to camouflage her while she sits on her nest.

**DID YOU KNOW?**
The heaviest ever domestic turkey weighed 86 lb—as much as a 12-year-old child.

# Megapodes and guans

- **There are more than 20 species of megapodes**—ground-living birds found in Australia and some Pacific islands. Megapode means "large foot."

- **The mallee fowl** (a megapode) lays its eggs in a huge mound of rotting leaves and sand, which acts as an incubator. The mound can be up to 36 ft across and 16.5 ft high.

- **One megapode in Tonga** makes a nest of warm volcanic sands and soil, which keeps its eggs warm.

- **The male mallee fowl** checks the temperature of its nest mounds with its beak and keeps it a constant 91.4°F by adding or removing material.

- **Mallee fowl chicks** must dig their way out of their nest mound, and are able to fly a few hours later.

- **To attract females**, the male crested guan flaps its wings briefly at over twice the normal speed, making a whirring sound as it flies.

▼ *The male mallee fowl keeps a constant watch over its nest.*

- **Now rare**, the white-winged guan lives in the Andean foothills, feeding on fruit, berries, leaves, and insects.

- **The 45 species of guan and curassow** live from southern U.S. to northern Argentina.

- **The great curassow** is 37.4 in long and weighs 10.6 lb.

- **True to its name**, the nocturnal curassow comes out at night to sing and feed on fruit.

- **The plain chachalaca** (curassow family) lays three eggs in a nest made of sticks and lined with leaves and moss.

▲ The curassow is a ground-dwelling forest bird, feeding on seeds, berries, and small animals.

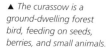

◄ The crested guan lives in the forests of Central America. It lives mainly in trees and walks or runs along the branches to look for wild figs, berries, and leaves to eat.

287

# Mesites and relatives

- **Mesites are thrushlike birds** that search for insects on the forest floor. They do have wings, but rarely fly.

- **Three species of mesite** live on the island of Madagascar, but they are all rare and threatened by habitat destruction.

- **The 15 species of button quail** live in parts of Europe, Africa, Asia, Australia, and some Pacific islands, usually on grassland. Although they look like quails, they are not related.

- **Shy little birds**, button quails lurk among low-growing plants feeding on seeds and insects.

- **The female button quail** is larger than the male. It mates with several males and leaves each to incubate the clutch of eggs and rear the young.

- **Button quail young** can fly two weeks after hatching, and start to breed when only four to five months old.

◄ *The little button quail lives in southern Europe, Africa, and parts of Asia. It is 5–6 in long.*

▲ *The secretive white-breasted mesite searches for insects among the leaves on the forest floor. It lives in family groups, resting in the shade during the day and perching on low branches at night.*

**Button quails** are sometimes known as hemipode, or half-footed, quails, because they lack rear toes.

**The plains-wanderer** lives on the dry plains of central Australia. If in danger, it stays very still.

**Plains-wanderers** are now rare because so much of the grassland where they live and feed has been cleared for agriculture. There may be fewer than 8,000 left in the wild.

**The female plains-wanderer** lays four eggs, usually in a nest made in a hollow on the ground, but it is the male that incubates the eggs and rears the young.

289

# Cranes and trumpeters

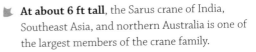

- **The 15 or so species of crane** live all over the world, in North America, Africa, Europe, Asia, and Australia.

- **In China and Japan** the crane symbolizes long life and good luck.

- **The crowned crane**, which has a fine crest of yellow feathers, performs a spectacular courtship display that involves leaping 6 ft into the air.

- **At about 6 ft tall**, the Sarus crane of India, Southeast Asia, and northern Australia is one of the largest members of the crane family.

- **The sandhill crane** makes a nest of plant material on the ground. The female lays two eggs, which both parents help to incubate. Soon after hatching, the young leave the nest.

- **Siberian cranes** have been known to live for more than 80 years. One captive male even fathered chicks at the age of 78!

- **The whooping crane** is the rarest crane in North America. It is named after its loud whooping or trumpeting call.

◄ *Like all cranes, Sarus cranes mate for life. They perform elaborate courtship dances, leaping into the air, bowing, tossing grass or sticks, stretching up their necks, and trumpeting loudly.*

- **The three species of trumpeter** live in tropical rain forests. All make loud trumpeting calls.

- **Trumpeters** spend most of their time on the ground searching for fruit, nuts, and insects, but they roost in trees.

- **The limpkin** is a relative of the cranes and the only member of its family. It has a long, curved beak, which it uses to remove snails from their shells.

▲ *Cranes fly with their necks stretched forward and their legs held straight out beyond their short tails.*

# Bustards

- **The 22 species** of bustard live in Africa, southern Europe, Asia, and Australia.

- **Bustards are large birds** with long legs. They live on the ground in deserts and open, grassy places.

- **These heavy birds** rely on hiding or running away from predators instead of flying. Their mottled brown feathers provide good camouflage.

- **Female great bustards** are usually much smaller and lighter than males, weighing only about 11 lb.

▼ A great bustard taking off from a field shows its enormous wingspan of up to 8 ft. This is probably the world's heaviest flying bird.

- **In the breeding season**, male great bustards compete for females at special display grounds called leks.

- **Male great bustards** display together, puffing out their chests with air, raising and spreading their tails over their backs, and revealing white rosettes of feathers.

- **Male crested bustards** perform spectacular "rocket flights," during which they fly vertically into the air for about 100 ft, then puff out their breast feathers, turn upside down, and drop vertically back down to the ground again.

- **To impress females**, male Bengal floricans (a type of bustard) leap up to 33 ft in the air during their courtship displays.

- **Pairs of Vigor's bustards** take part in croaking duets. Their calls carry long distances.

- **Little bustards** are short, chunky birds, which weigh less than 2.2 lb.

▶ The kori bustard lives on the African plains, eating insects, seeds, berries, small mammals, lizards, and snakes. Males may weigh up to 39 lb, which is twice as much as the females.

293

# Ostriches and emus

🦃 **The ostrich** is the largest of all birds alive today. It stands 8.2 ft tall and weighs about 286 lb—more than twice as much as an average human.

🦃 **The male ostrich** makes a shallow nest on the ground and mates with several females, all of whom lay their eggs in the nest. The chief female incubates the eggs during the day, and the male takes over at night.

🦃 **Ostriches** don't really bury their heads in the sand. But if a female is approached by an enemy while sitting on the nest, she will press her long neck flat on the ground to appear less obvious.

🦃 **Ostrich chicks** have many enemies, including jackals and hyenas. Only 15 percent are likely to survive until they are one year old.

🦃 **In Southwest Asia**, the shells of ostrich eggs are believed to have magical powers. They are sometimes placed on the roofs of houses as protection from evil.

🦃 **The largest bird** in Australia is the emu, which measures 6 ft tall and weighs as much as 99 lb. Like the ostrich, it cannot fly.

🦃 **Seeds, fruits, flowers, and plant shoots** are an emu's main sources of food, but it also eats some insects and small animals.

🦃 **The male emu** incubates its mate's clutch of eggs for eight weeks, during which time it does not eat or drink. It lives on the stores of body fat that it has built up during the previous months.

🦃 **An emu's feathers** are each made up of two quills, which are the same length.

**DID YOU KNOW?**
Emus can sprint at speeds of up to 30 mph and make long leaps over distances of up to 8.8 ft.

▼ Ostriches live in Africa, in dry grassland areas. They often have to run long distances in search of food.

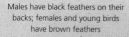

Males have black feathers on their backs; females and young birds have brown feathers

Long, flexible neck is bare of feathers

Long, strong legs for running

295

# Cassowaries and kiwis

- **There are three species of kiwi**, found only in New Zealand. All are flightless birds that live in burrows.

- **Largest of its family is the brown kiwi**, which is about 21 in long and weighs up to 8 lb.

- **Only the kiwi** has nostrils at the end of its beak.

▼ *The nocturnal kiwi's good sense of smell helps it to find worms, insects, and spiders in the ground at night.*

## DID YOU KNOW?

A kiwi lays the largest eggs for its size of any bird—each egg weighs 25 percent of its body weight. Females lay up to 100 in a lifetime.

- **The kiwi** is the national symbol of New Zealand, appearing on stamps, coins, and bank notes.

- **About 94 percent** of the chicks of the northern brown kiwi die before they are able to breed. Major threats include introduced predators, such as stoats and cats.

- **Cassowaries** in Australia are known to eat the fruits of 75 different types of tree.

- **The female cassowary** mates with several males, laying six to eight eggs each time. The males care for the young.

- **The female dwarf cassowary**, or moruk, is an extremely dangerous bird and will attack anything that comes near its nest with its 4-in-long claws.

- **During his courtship display**, the male double-wattled cassowary circles the female, using its inflated throat pouch to make booming sounds.

▼ Cassowaries use the tall, horny casques on their heads to push aside the tangled undergrowth in their rain forest home. Their long, hairlike feathers protect their skin from scratches.

# Rheas and tinamous

- **The largest bird in South America** is the greater rhea, which stands 5 ft tall and weighs up to 55 lb.

- **Rheas feed mostly on plants**, but will also eat insects and even lizards when they can.

- **Flocks of rheas** can number between five and 50 birds.

- **If threatened**, a rhea lies flat on the ground with its head stretched out in an attempt to hide.

- **Rhea feathers** are used to make feather dusters, for sale mainly in the U.S. and Japan.

- **The 45 or so species** of tinamou all live in Central and South America.

- **Most tinamous** can fly, if only for short distances, but they tend to run or hide rather than take to the air.

- **Tinamous** generally eat fruit, seeds, and other plant matter, but some species also eat insects.

- **Female tinamous** lay eggs in the nests of more than one male. Males incubate the eggs and feed the chicks.

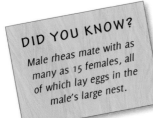

DID YOU KNOW?
Male rheas mate with as many as 15 females, all of which lay eggs in the male's large nest.

▶ Flocks of rheas live on the pampas grasslands and in open woodland in southeastern South America.

# Woodland and forest birds

# Toucans and honeyguides

🦜 **There are about 40 species of toucan.** They live in Mexico and Central and South America.

🦜 **Toucans feed** mostly on fruit, which they pluck from branches with their long beaks. They also eat some insects and small animals, such as lizards.

🦜 **Although a toucan's beak is large**, it is not heavy. The beak is made of a lightweight material with a honeycomb structure.

Beak is about 8 in long and 3 in deep at the base

🦜 **Toucans are noisy creatures**—their loud squawks can be heard half a mile away.

Strong claws for perching

▶ The toco toucan of Brazil is the best known of the toucans. It will sometimes perch on a branch near another bird's nest to steal the eggs or chicks. Intimidated by the toucan's great beak, the parent bird will not generally attack.

► The black-throated honeyguide is usually a quiet little bird, but it chatters noisily when it wants to attract a helper to a bees' nest.

🐾 **Toucans usually nest** in tree holes. The female lays two to four eggs and the male helps to incubate them, which takes about 15 days.

🐾 **When toucans first hatch,** they have spiky ankle pads, which help to protect their feet from the rough wood and piles of discarded seeds inside their nesting hole.

🐾 **At 24 in long**, the toco toucan is the largest toucan. Its colorful beak alone is up to 7.8 in long.

🐾 **There are about 15 species of honeyguide.** Most live in forests and woodlands in Africa, but there are a few species resident in Asia.

🐾 **Honeyguides are the only birds** that are able to feed on the wax from bees' nests, as well as on the insects themselves.

🐾 **The black-throated honeyguide** likes to feed on bees and their larvae. When it finds a bees' nest, it leads another creature, such as a honey badger, to the nest and waits while the animal breaks into the nest to feed on the honey. The honeyguide then has its share.

# Hornbills

▲ *The great Indian hornbill has a big yellow casque and a loud, roaring call. When it flies, its large wings make a "whooshing" sound.*

- **There are about** 57 species of hornbill—23 in Africa and 34 in Southeast Asia. Most live among trees.

- **Most hornbills** feed mainly on fruit, but the two ground hornbills catch and eat small animals.

- **All hornbills** have large beaks. In many species the beak is topped with a casque made of keratin and bone.

- **The helmeted hornbill** has a dense, ivorylike casque, which makes up about 10 percent of the bird's weight.

- **Hornbills are the only birds** in which two neck vertebrae are fused, possibly to help support the weight of the beak.

- **Hornbills range** from 12–47 in in size. The largest of the family is the southern ground hornbill and the smallest is the black dwarf hornbill.

- **Hornbills live** for 35–40 years in the wild and up to 50 years in captivity in zoos.

- **The eastern yellow-billed hornbill** and the dwarf mongoose have an unusual relationship—they help each other find food and watch out for predators.

- **In parts of South Africa**, the southern ground hornbill is traditionally considered sacred and is protected.

- **A male hornbill** may carry more than 60 small fruits at a time to its nest to regurgitate for its young.

▶ *The yellow-billed hornbill is 20 in long and lives in southern Africa.*

# Woodpeckers

◄ The great spotted woodpecker has red feathers under its tail and white shoulder patches. The male also has a red patch on the back of its head (nape).

The 200 or so species of woodpecker live all over the world, except in Antarctica, Madagascar, and Australia.

Woodpeckers feed by drilling into tree bark with their sharp beaks, and then inserting their long tongues into the holes to pick out insects living beneath the bark.

A woodpecker's tongue is well adapted for catching insects. It is so long that the woodpecker can stick it out beyond the tip of its beak. The tongue's sticky coating easily mops up prey.

Woodpeckers drum on tree trunks with their beaks to signal their ownership of territory or their readiness to mate. The great spotted woodpecker has been timed making 20 strikes a second.

Woodpeckers nest in holes in trees. They may use a hole from a previous year, or dig out a new one for their two to 12 eggs.

▶ The lesser spotted woodpecker is smaller than the great spotted and is not much bigger than a sparrow. The male has a red cap.

- **A woodpecker** may eat as many as 1,000 ants in one feeding session.

- **The imperial woodpecker** is thought to be critically endangered and may be extinct. At 21.6 in long, it is the biggest of its family, while the little scaled piculet is only 3 in long.

- **The sapsucker** (woodpecker family) feeds on sweet, sugary sap. It bores a hole in a tree and laps up the sap that oozes out.

- **As well as insects**, the great spotted woodpecker eats the eggs and young of other birds.

- **During the fall**, the acorn woodpecker of North America bores as many as 400 holes in tree trunks and puts an acorn in each one, to store for the winter.

▶ The red-bellied woodpecker feeds on wood-boring beetles, grasshoppers, and ants, as well as acorns, beechnuts, and wild fruits. It stores some food to help it survive the winter.

307

# Bee-eaters and relatives

- **The 27 species of bee-eater** are colorful birds that live in southern Europe, Africa, Asia, and Australia.

- **Bee-eaters** catch bees or wasps and kill them by striking them against branches. The birds rub the insects against the branches to get rid of their stings.

- **The European bee-eater** flies some 10,000 mi between Europe, where it breeds, and Africa, where it overwinters.

- **The ten species of motmot** live only in forests stretching from Mexico to northern Argentina.

▶ *White-fronted bee-eaters feed mainly on bees, but also catch other flying insects, such as butterflies.*

**DID YOU KNOW?**
A European bee-eater eats about 200 bees a day. Its summer diet is mainly bumblebees, and in winter it eats honeybees and dragonflies.

▲ *The carmine bee-eater often digs nesting burrows in vertical sandy banks. Nesting colonies may contain hundreds or even thousands of pairs of birds.*

**Motmots range in size** from the 7.5-in-long tody motmot to the 21-in-long upland motmot.

**Motmots lay their eggs** in chambers at the ends of burrows dug in earth banks. Both parents incubate the eggs and feed the chicks.

**The blue-crowned motmot** has two long tail feathers with racquet-shaped tips. The bird swings its tail like a clock's pendulum as it watches for prey.

**Todies** nest in 12-in-long tunnels, which they dig with their beaks.

**The five species of tody** are all insect-eating birds that live in the tropical Caribbean islands.

# Swifts

- **There are about 100 species of swift** found all over the world, except in the far north and far south.

- **Swifts do almost everything** in the air. They eat, drink, court, and sometimes even sleep on the wing.

- **Trials with ringed birds** have shown that a young common swift that has only just left the nest can fly from London to Madrid in three days.

- **A swift's legs and feet** are so small and weak that it cannot move on the ground. It must land on a cliff ledge or building so it can launch itself into the air again.

- **Swifts regurgitate** mouthfuls of food for their young to eat. Each mouthful may contain hundreds or thousands of tiny insects and spiders.

- **Once a young swift** has left the nest, it may not come to land again until it is about three or four years old and ready to breed.

▶ The common or Eurasian swift is often seen in Europe in the summer, swooping overhead as it hunts for insects. It flies to tropical Africa for the winter.

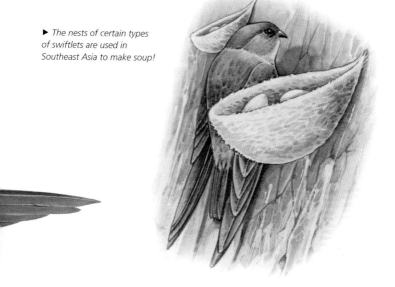

▶ The nests of certain types
of swiftlets are used in
Southeast Asia to make soup!

- **The largest swift**, the white-naped swift, is about 10 in long and weighs 6 oz—about the weight of a lemon.

- **The African palm swift** glues its nest to the underneath of a palm leaf with its own spit, and glues its eggs to the nest. The parents cling on with their claws while incubating the clutch.

- **The edible-nest swiftlet** makes a nest of its own spit and a few feathers on a cave wall. Soup made from these nests is considered a great delicacy in Asia.

- **The cave swiftlet** finds its way in totally dark caves by using a form of echolocation.

# Cuckoos and relatives

- **The Eurasian cuckoo** is a "brood parasite"—it lays its eggs in the nests of other birds.

- **A female Eurasian cuckoo** removes an egg from another bird's nest before laying her own.

- **Most birds** take several minutes to lay an egg, but the cuckoo lays one in just ten seconds, so it can quickly take advantage of any brief absence of the host bird.

- **The eggs of brood parasite cuckoos** vary in color and markings according to the host they use. A Eurasian cuckoo's eggs may resemble those of reed warblers, garden warblers, or redstarts.

- **Of the 140 or so species of cuckoo**, only about 59 lay their eggs in other birds' nests.

- **The hoatzin** is 23 in long and lives deep in South America's rain forest.

- **Hoatzin chicks** leave the nest soon after hatching. Two little claws on each of their wings help them clamber about.

▶ The hoatzin, from northern South America, has a large plume on its head and, unlike other birds, feeds almost entirely on leaves.

▶ The Eurasian cuckoo has a long, rounded tail and pointed wings. Young cuckoos have more rounded wings, like those of owls.

- **The 22 species** of turaco live only in Africa. Largest is the 30-in-long great blue turaco, weighing 2.2 lb.

- **Turacos feed mostly** on fruit, leaves, and flowers, but also catch some insects in the breeding season.

- **The Australian koel** prefers fruit to the creatures, such as caterpillars, eaten by other cuckoos.

▼ These flycatchers are busy feeding a cuckoo chick in their nest.

313

# Kingfishers

- **The 90 or so species of kingfisher** are found all over the world, except parts of the far north.

- **The giant kingfisher** of Africa and the Australian laughing kookaburra (a kingfisher) are the largest of the family, at about 18 in long.

- **The common kingfisher** nests at the end of a 3-ft-long tunnel that it excavates in a riverbank. The female lays four to eight eggs.

- **Common kingfishers** incubate their eggs for 19–21 days and feed the young for up to four weeks.

▼ *The river kingfisher fiercely defends the stretch of riverbank where it feeds and nests.*

◄ *The tiny pygmy kingfisher is only 4.7 in long. It lives in the woodlands and forests of Africa.*

**A flash of iridescent** turquoise feathers streaking at high speed along a quiet riverbank indicates the presence of a common or European kingfisher.

**The African pygmy kingfisher** feeds mainly on dry land, diving down from a perch to catch insects, spiders, millipedes, and even small frogs and lizards.

**The shovel-billed kingfisher** is armed with its own spade for digging in mud—it uses its large, heavy bill to dig up worms, shellfish, and small reptiles.

**In the forests of New Guinea**, the male paradise kingfisher shows off its long tail feathers to females as part of its courtship display.

**The laughing kookaburra** is named for its call, which sounds like noisy laughter. It makes its call to claim territory. Once one starts, others tend to join in!

**In northern Australia**, termite mounds are adopted as nest sites by the buff-breasted kingfisher.

315

# Nightjars and relatives

- **There are about 70 species** of nightjar, which live in most parts of the world, especially in the tropics.

- **An old name for nightjars** is goatsuckers, because people mistakenly thought they saw the birds feeding on goats' milk, when in fact they were snapping up insects disturbed by the animals.

- **The bristle-fringed beak** of the nightjar opens very wide to help it snap up moths and beetles at night.

- **After hunting for insects** at night, the common potoo rests by day in a tree, where its coloration makes it look like a broken branch.

- **The 12 species of frogmouth** live in the rain forests of Southeast Asia and Australia.

- **The common poorwill** is one of the few birds known to hibernate. It sleeps in a rock crevice.

- **The oilbird** is the only bird to feed on fruit at night. Its excellent sense of smell helps it find the oily fruits of palms and laurels in the dark.

◀ *The potoo lives in forests and woodlands in Mexico and Central and South America.*

**DID YOU KNOW?**

Potoos can squirt their feces away from their perches, so they do not mark their hiding places for a predator to find.

▲ *Nightjars are active fliers but rest on the ground during the day, where they are well camouflaged.*

- **Oilbird chicks** put on so much weight from their rich diet that they may weigh much more than their parents when they are only a couple of months old.

- **The oilbird nests** in dark caves and uses echolocation to aid navigation.

317

# Jacamars and relatives

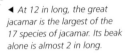

◀ At 12 in long, the great jacamar is the largest of the 17 species of jacamar. Its beak alone is almost 2 in long.

- **Jacamars live** in Central and South America.

- **They nest in tunnels** made in the ground or in termite mounds, and lay two to four eggs, which they incubate for 20–23 days.

- **A jacamar** snaps up an insect in the air, then returns to its perch and bangs the insect against a branch to kill it before eating it.

- **Brightly colored barbets** live in tropical forests and woodlands in Africa, Asia, and South America.

- **Biggest of the 83 species of barbet** is the toucan barbet, at 7.8 in long. It lives in mountain forests in the northern part of South America.

- **The double-toothed barbet** is named after the two sharp points on the top part of its bill.

- **Many barbet** pairs sing together to keep their relationship close. One bird starts to sing, then stops, and the other bird continues the song within a fraction of a second.

- **There are about 35 species of puffbird** living in Mexico and Central and South America.

- **The white-fronted nunbird** (puffbird family) digs a nesting burrow about 3 ft long. The bird lays its eggs in a chamber at the end of the burrow.

**DID YOU KNOW?**

At night, the white-whiskered puffbird seals the entrance to its nest burrow with green leaves.

▶ The crested barbet of southern Africa usually searches for food on the ground. It roosts in holes in trees.

# Pigeons and sandgrouse

- **There are more than 300 species** of pigeon, and they occur all over the world, except in the far north and Antarctica.

- **Pigeons and doves** can suck up water when they drink. This is unique among birds—all other birds have to tip their heads back to drink.

- **Both male and female pigeons** can make a milky substance in their crops, which they feed to their young.

- **Wood pigeons** feed on leaves, seeds, nuts, berries, and some insects. Those living near humans also eat bread and food scraps.

- **The dark green feathers** of the African green pigeon provide good camouflage in its forest home, especially when it keeps very still.

◄ Domesticated pigeons are descended from the wild rock dove. These pigeons were first domesticated in Iraq over 6,000 years ago.

▲ The Namaqua sandgrouse of southern Africa flies up to 50 mi a day in search of food and water in its dry grassland and desert habitat.

**DID YOU KNOW?**
The full crop of a Namaqua sandgrouse contains between 3,000 and 40,000 seeds.

- **At 27.5–29.5 in long** (nearly as big as a turkey), the Victoria crowned pigeon of New Guinea is the largest member of its family.

- **Pigeon "races"** are held in which birds return to their homes from 600 mi away.

- **The 16 or so species** of sandgrouse live in southern Europe, Africa, and parts of Asia. They are not related to true grouse, even though they look rather like them.

- **Sandgrouse are suited** to extreme desert conditions, withstanding soaring temperatures with little need for water. They are strong fliers and travel long distances to find water.

321

# Hummingbirds

▶ *The sword-billed hummingbird uses its extraordinary bill to reach deep inside trumpet-shaped flowers and feed on the insects and nectar.*

- **The 320 or so species of hummingbird** live in North, Central, and South America. Largest is the giant hummingbird, at about 8 in long and weighing 0.7 oz.

- **A hummingbird** hovers in front of flowers to collect nectar with its tongue, which has a brushlike tip.

- **Hummingbirds** are the only birds able to fly backward as well as forward while they are hovering.

- **To fuel its energy needs**, a hummingbird must eat at least half its weight in food each day.

- **Hummingbirds are so active** that their hearts beat more than 1,200 times a minute.

- **The bee hummingbird** is not much bigger than a bumblebee and, at 2.4 in long, is probably the smallest bird.

- **A hovering bee hummingbird** beats its wings 80 times a second.

- **At 4.1 in**, the beak of the sword-billed hummingbird is longer than the rest of its body.

- **Tiny ruby-throated hummingbirds** migrate each fall from the U.S., across the Gulf of Mexico, to Central America. Although only 3.5 in long, the bird flies at a speed of about 27 mph.

- **The female calliope hummingbird** lays two tiny eggs in a nest made of lichen, moss, and spiders' webs. She incubates the eggs for 15 days and feeds the young for about 20 days, until they are able to fly and find food for themselves.

▲ The male ruby-throated hummingbird courts its mate by flying back and forth in a wide arc, like a pendulum, while making a loud humming sound. The female may join in the display.

323

# More hummingbirds

- **Hummingbirds** have the fewest feathers of any birds—about 1,000–1,500 in total.

- **A hummingbird's flight muscles** make up 25–30 percent of its overall weight.

- **The average lifespan** of hummingbirds in the wild is three to 12 years.

- **Despite their size**, hummingbirds will chase away rivals or attack large predators, such as jays, crows, and hawks.

- **The starling-sized giant hummingbird** from the Andes lets its body temperature fall at night to save energy.

- **The marvellous spatuletail hummingbird** has only four tail feathers, whereas most hummingbirds have ten. Two of the male's tail feathers finish in a broad, flat end, or "spatule," and are used in its courtship display.

- **Male long-tailed hermits** (a type of hummingbird) gather in singing groups called leks, and compete with each other to attract mates.

▼ *The crimson topaz hummingbird feeds on flowers high up in the canopy of the Amazon rain forest. The male (shown here) is more colorful than the female and has long tail feathers that cross over half way down.*

**Male streamertails** (Jamaican hummingbirds) wave their long black tail feathers from side to side during their courtship displays.

**Bearded helmetcrest hummingbirds** are well camouflaged in their forest habitat, but only the male has a black crest and a white, green, and black "beard" of feathers.

**Puffleg hummingbirds** look as if they are wearing feather "muffs" on their legs. The color of these leg muffs varies in different species.

325

# Hoopoes and relatives

- **The eight noisy, insect-eating woodhoopoe** species live in forests in central and southern Africa.

- **Groups of woodhoopoes** make loud calls and rocking movements, and pass bark to each other, in a display of territorial ownership.

- **If threatened by a bird of prey**, the hoopoe hides by flattening itself on the ground with its wings and tail spread out.

- **The hoopoe** is named after its characteristic "hoo-poo-poo" call, which carries over long distances. Hoopoes often live near people and hunt for worms and grubs in gardens.

▶ With its decorative crest and striking plumage, the hoopoe is easy to recognize. It lives in Europe, Asia, and Africa.

- **The hoopoe** lines its nest with animal excrement, perhaps so that the smell will keep enemies away!

- **The 16 or so species of roller** and ground roller live in southern Europe, Asia, Africa, and Australia.

- **Rollers** have spectacular courtship flights, rolling and somersaulting as they dive toward land.

- **A light, coin-shaped mark** on each wing of the broad-billed roller is the reason for its other common name—"dollar bird."

- **The cuckoo-roller** lives only in Madagascar and the Comoros Islands, where it catches chameleons and insects.

- **The broad-billed roller** catches winged termites in the air. A roller will eat as many as 800 termites in a single evening.

▶ *Rollers use a diving method of hunting that is typical of this group of birds. They catch their prey in midair or by swooping to the ground.*

327

# Mousebirds and trogons

**The six species of mousebird** are all small, dull-colored birds that are not related to trogons. They live in Africa to the south of the Sahara.

**Mousebirds** are named for their habit of scurrying around on the ground like mice, as they search for seeds and leaves to eat.

**Mousebirds** are plant eaters, feeding on a variety of leaves, buds, flowers, and fruits.

**There are about 37 species of trogon** living in the forests and woodlands of Central America, the Caribbean islands, and parts of Africa and Asia.

**Trogons range in size** from the black-throated trogon, at 9 in long, to the resplendent quetzal, which measures 13 in long.

**Trogons nest in tree holes**, old termite mounds, or wasps' nests. Both parents incubate the two to four eggs for 17–19 days and take care of the young.

◀ *The beautiful quetzal is becoming rare because much of its forest habitat in Central America has been destroyed.*

- **Insects are the main food** of trogons, but some also eat fruit and catch creatures, such as lizards.

- **The quetzal** is a species of trogon that lives in Central America. It was sacred to the ancient Maya and Aztec civilizations.

- **The male quetzal's** beautiful tail feathers are up to 3 ft long.

◀ *Trogons have a wide, hooked bill, which is surrounded by bristles that help them to catch flying insects.*

**DID YOU KNOW?**

The monetary unit of Guatemala is known as the quetzal, after the resplendent quetzal—the country's national bird.

329

# People and birds

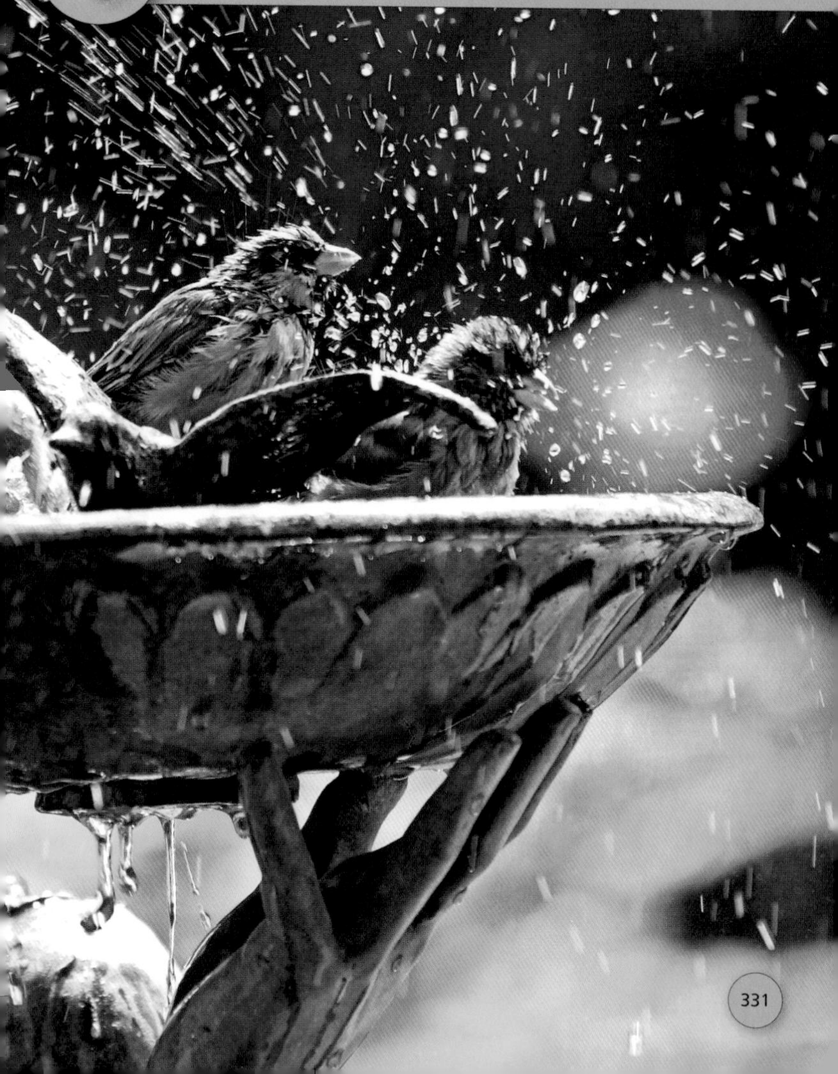

# Myths and legends

- **There are many superstitions** about ravens—the arrival of a raven is said to be an evil omen and a sign of an imminent death.

- **The ibis** was a symbol of the god Thoth in ancient Egypt, and appears in many paintings and carvings. Mummified ibises have also been discovered—as many as 500,000 in one tomb.

- **Ostrich feathers** were used as symbols of justice in ancient Egypt.

- **The hoopoe** was a symbol of gratitude in ancient Egyptian hieroglyphics. The Egyptians believed that the hoopoe comforted its parents in their old age.

- **The ancient Egyptian god Horus**, god of the sky and heavens, was often depicted with the head of a falcon.

- **In Greek mythology**, the harpy had the body of an eagle and the head of a woman. These winged monsters brought violent winds.

- **The little owl** was the sacred bird of the ancient Greek goddess of wisdom, Athena.

- **The Gandaberunda** (or Berunda) is a two-headed bird from Hindu mythology, believed to possess magical strength and often carved on Hindu temples.

◄ Horus, the falcon-headed god of ancient Egypt, was a peregrine falcon. His red and white crown is a symbol of his power over the two parts of the kingdom of Egypt.

**DID YOU KNOW?**
A gigantic, legendary bird of prey called the Roc, or Rukh, was said to be strong enough to carry three elephants in its claws.

- **In Norse mythology**, a pair of ravens called Hugin (thought) and Munin (Memory) brought news and information to the god Odin.

- **The phoenix** is a sacred firebird, which features in the myths of the Phoenicians, Egyptians, and Greeks. It lives for 500–1,000 years, after which it burns in a nest of twigs. A new young phoenix, or phoenix egg, appears in the ashes. The ancient Egyptians associated the phoenix with immortality.

▶ A griffin is a legendary creature with the head of an eagle, the body of a lion, and the wings of a dragon. In mythology, it is known for guarding treasure.

333

# Birds in history

🦅 **Falconry is the art** of using birds of prey to catch wild animals. Originally it was a means of providing food, but it became more of a status symbol for the rich nobles of Europe in medieval society.

🦅 **Falconry probably began** in central Asia and the Middle East, perhaps as long ago as 1000 BC or even 2000 BC. Falconry is shown in some of the oldest wall paintings from ancient Egypt.

🦅 **The ancient Greeks** used pigeons to carry the names of the victors of the Olympic Games to various cities in Greece.

🦅 **In ancient Rome**, peacocks were roasted and served in their feathers as a great delicacy.

🦅 **In heraldry**, a pelican is shown pecking its breast to feed its young on its blood. This may stem from the bird's habit of resting its beak on its breast.

🦅 **Some medieval falcons** were so valuable that they were used in ransom negotiations. They were worth more than their weight in gold.

🦅 **King Henry VIII** was very keen on falconry and is said to have kept 100 albino falcons.

A falconer pulls the hood off using the top knot

Hood braces are gently pulled to tighten the hood on the bird's head

◀ *Falconers use a leather head covering (hood) to keep their birds calm. The birds are less likely to become agitated if they can't see the world around them.*

DID YOU KNOW?

In Christianity, a dove is often used to symbolize the Holy Spirit. Doves are often released as a gesture of peace and goodwill.

🐦 **In Tudor England**, the type of falcon a person was allowed to fly depended on their rank in society. A king flew a peregrine falcon and a lady flew a merlin, while a servant could only fly a kestrel.

🐦 **In the 19th century**, grebes' breast feathers were used to make muffs to keep ladies' hands warm.

🐦 **Canaries were once used** in British coal mines as an early warning system. Toxic gases in the mine tunnels would kill the birds before it affected the miners themselves.

Bells are attached to the bird's legs, tail, or neck, allowing a falconer to keep track of his or her bird

▶ A selection of the equipment, called "furniture," used by falconers. There are many different designs and some species or individuals have different equipment needs.

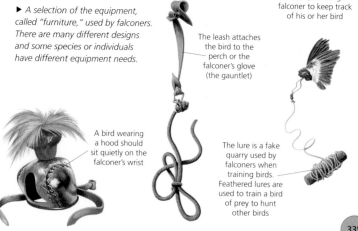

The leash attaches the bird to the perch or the falconer's glove (the gauntlet)

A bird wearing a hood should sit quietly on the falconer's wrist

The lure is a fake quarry used by falconers when training birds. Feathered lures are used to train a bird of prey to hunt other birds

335

# Birds in literature

- **Edward Lear**, an English artist, author, and poet, wrote his celebrated poem *The Owl and the Pussycat* in 1867 for the children of his patron, Edward Stanley, the 13th Earl of Derby.

- **A dodo features** in *Alice in Wonderland* by Lewis Carroll. Carroll's real name was Charles Lutwidge Dodgson, and he intended the dodo to be a caricature of himself—he had a slight stutter and sometimes pronounced his name "Do-do-Dodgson."

- **Other birds** in *Alice in Wonderland* include the flamingo, which Alice uses as a mallet for playing croquet, and the lory and eaglet, said to be based on Alice's sisters, Lorina and Edith.

- **In *The Last Battle***, the final book in C. S. Lewis' *The Chronicles of Narnia* series, Farsight the eagle brings news to Tirian, the last king of Narnia.

- **In the *Harry Potter* stories** by J. K. Rowling, owls carry messages for the witches and wizards. Harry has a snowy owl called Hedwig, Ron Weasley has a scops owl called Pigwidgeon, and the Weasley family's post owl is a great gray owl called Errol.

▶ The owl plays a guitar in a "pea-green boat" in Edward Lear's famous nonsense poem, The Owl and the Pussycat.

- In ***The Phoenix and the Carpet*** by E. Nesbit, some children find a phoenix egg in a carpet. When it hatches, the phoenix explains that the carpet will grant the children wishes every day, taking them on a series of adventures.

- ***The Rime of the Ancient Mariner***, by the English Poet Samuel Taylor Coleridge, tells of a mariner (sailor) who brings bad luck to his ship by killing an albatross.

- In ***The Happy Prince***, Oscar Wilde describes how a swallow takes jewels and gold from the statue of a prince to help those in need and bring happiness to others.

- In his fairy tale *The Ugly Duckling*, the Danish poet and author Hans Christian Andersen wrote of the unhappiness and ill-treatment of an ugly swan cygnet, before it changed into a beautiful swan.

- **Set against** the background of World War II, *The Snow Goose* by Paul Gallico tells the story of a disabled painter who lives in a lighthouse, and the girl who brings him an injured snow goose.

▼ *The ugly "duckling" was really a swan cygnet, which hatched out of a swan's egg that rolled into a duck's nest by mistake.*

337

# Watching birds

▪ **Keen eyes, stealth, and patience** are the most useful qualities in a birdwatcher.

▪ **Always avoid** disturbing birds, particularly if they have eggs or young. Move quietly, slowly, and carefully, wear dull-colored clothes, and try to blend in with the scenery.

▪ **Try to approach birds** with the wind blowing in your face. Then the sounds you make will not carry so easily to the birds and frighten them away.

▪ **Never touch** or collect eggs or nests. If you see a baby bird on its own, it is best to leave it alone. One of its parents is probably nearby and will soon be back with some food.

▼ *At Hawk Mountain, Pennsylvannia, U.S., birdwatchers have the chance to observe large numbers of hawks, eagles, and falcons as they fly past on their migration journeys.*

**DID YOU KNOW?**

The best time to look for birds is soon after dawn or just before dusk.

- **Get to know the birds** in your garden or street first. Then explore the local park, a lake, or a river, and eventually try open country. Always tell someone where you are going, and check the tides if you go birdwatching on the coast.

- **For serious birdwatching**, you really need a pair of binoculars. These should be light enough to carry around and have good magnification, together with a fairly wide field of view. One of the best binoculars for general birdwatching are 8 x 30 (8=magnification; 30=diameter of the lens).

- **Telescopes (often with tripods)** are more powerful than binoculars and they are used by many birdwatching enthusiasts and in wildlife centers. Lenses of 60–70 mm are ideal as they let enough light into the telescope to produce a detailed image. A telescope can be focused on a particular bird or nest site so that different people can see the bird easily.

- **The best cover** for birdwatching is a hide, which can be made of a material such as canvas, painted with green and brown blotches for camouflage, and draped on a frame of sticks or poles. Vertical slits in the hide make good viewing holes.

- **A car makes a good hide**, if it is driven slowly to a place near the birds and the people inside keep quiet and still.

# Identifying birds

🪶 **One of the most important items** for a birdwatcher is a field notebook in which to record details of the birds that he or she sees.

🪶 **Every entry in a field notebook** should include the date, the place where the bird was seen, the time of day, and the weather conditions.

🪶 **Keep a note** of the sort of habitat the bird lives in, such as woodland, shoreline, marsh, grassland, and so on.

🪶 **Small sketches of the birds** will help you remember the shape of the bird and its distinctive colors and markings.

🪶 **To sketch a land bird**, draw two circles, one for the head and one for the body, and leave a gap between them. Add the neck, bill, and legs, and fill in the pattern of the feathers last.

🪶 **To sketch a water bird**, use a half circle for the body and a small circle for the head.

◀ *A page from a birdwatcher's notebook shows the field notes made to help them identify a chiffchaff.*

▼ ▶ Field guides are a great help with bird identification. They label a bird's characteristic colors and markings, which help to distinguish one species from another.

SPOT 50 Garden Birds

How to identify 50 species

**BULLFINCH**

Bullfinches are often seen in couples, and are thought to pair for life. They are shy and secretive birds, and like to stay close to cover. The bullfinch rarely forages on the ground, and is usually spotted in trees and bushes, using its strong beak to harvest seeds, berries and buds. In autumn and early winter these birds feed on seeds, such as ash keys.

SCALE

FACT FILE
Scientific name
Pyrrhula pyrrhula
Size 15 cm
Wingspan 22-26 cm
Call Distinct, low, piping 'pheeo'
Breeding Two broods, 4-6 eggs
April to June

Bullfinches are rosy at the bird table, but they will take shelled peanuts from a net.

Black cap

Stubby, black bill

White rump

Rosy red breast

**CHAFFINCH**

Male chaffinches have rosy pink breasts and cheeks with bluish-grey heads. Females have greenish-brown backs and greyish-brown feathers underneath. Chaffinches differ from one region to another. They eat fruit, insects and seeds that they find on the ground, but they also catch insects in flight.

Chaffinches build their cup-shaped nests with grasses, mosses and lichens in the fork of a tree. The nests are lined with feathers and joined with spiders' webs.

FACT
Scientific na
Si
Wing
Call Loud
Breeding
April, m

Bands of white on wings

Pink chest feathers

Brown tail

Black crown

Bright yellow wing bars

Black chin

Green yellow breast

Grey-white underneath

- **Draw simple sketches** of what the bird looks like in flight, when you may see different colors and patterns on the wings and body. Start with two circles, then add the wings, tail, neck, and bill.

- **A bird's behavior** provides valuable clues to its identity, so jot down information such as how it feeds, how it reacts to other birds, how it moves, and how it displays to a rival or a mate.

- **You may be able** to record bird calls or songs, or take a short film of the birds you are watching to study later.

- **A lightweight field guide** will help you to identify birds when you are out and about, or allow you to identify birds from your field notebook after a birdwatching trip.

341

# Parts of a bird

- **Being able to name** the parts of a bird helps birdwatchers to take quick and accurate notes in the field.

- **Using the correct terms** for bird parts also helps birdwatchers to compare birds they have seen, and to check the variations in color and pattern within a species.

- **The lore** is the area on a bird's head between the base of the upper bill and the eye.

- **A superciliary stripe** is a streak of contrasting feathers above a bird's eye.

- **The feathers** overlying the bases of the tail feathers or major wing feathers are called coverts. The area of feathers covering a bird's ear is called the ear covert.

▼ *Mallards have a violet-blue speculum, outlined in white. This is most obvious when these ducks spread their wing feathers in flight.*

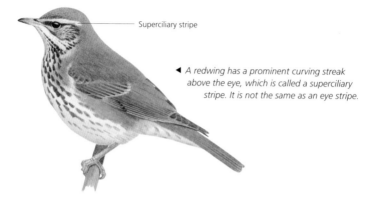

Superciliary stripe

◀ A redwing has a prominent curving streak above the eye, which is called a superciliary stripe. It is not the same as an eye stripe.

🪶 **The flight feathers** attached to a bird's "forearm" are called secondary feathers or secondaries.

🪶 **A speculum** is a contrasting patch of secondary feathers in the wing, usually in ducks.

🪶 **A bird's main flight feathers** are called primaries. They are attached to its "hand."

🪶 **The cere** is a fleshy covering at the base of the bill, which occurs in birds such as hawks, pigeons, or budgerigars.

🪶 **The feathers** above a bird's shoulders are called scapulars.

🪶 **The feathers** between a bird's neck and back are called the mantle.

Cere

▶ A pigeon's cere (waxlike "saddle" at the top of the bill) is white in adults, but grayish in young birds. The cere helps to protect the nostrils and plays a role in breathing.

343

# Birds in flight

- **Different species of birds** have different flight patterns, which are related to their wing shapes and the way they live and feed. Even when a bird is too far away for you to see it clearly, noticing details of its flight pattern may help you to identify it.

- **Wood pigeons clap their wings together** in flight to warn others of danger, or as part of their courtship display flights.

- **Some birds**, such as seagulls and vultures, soar on rising currents of hot air (thermals) without flapping their wings.

- **A few birds**, such as hummingbirds and kestrels, can hover in one spot. Kestrels hover high in the air to search for small rodents on the ground below, while hummingbirds hover to feed at flowers.

- **Birds with narrow, pointed wings**, such as swallows and swifts, are fast fliers. A swift alternates fast beats of its wings with short glides, often twisting and turning in the air.

- **A green woodpecker** has a distinctive bouncing flight. It rises and falls in the air as it flaps and then closes its broad wings.

- **A heron's flight silhouette** is easy to recognize. It flies slowly, with its huge wings curved downward, keeping its head drawn well back and leaving its legs trailing behind.

- **Owls fly slowly and silently** on their long, broad wings. Sometimes they glide and wheel in the air at dusk as they search the ground for prey.

- **The big, wide, rounded wings** of pheasants and other gamebirds are adapted for short, fast flight, allowing them to escape danger.

▶ Ducks, such as this mallard, flap their wings all the time when they fly. A mallard has a slower wingbeat than most ducks, but is a fast flier, reaching top speeds of 60 mph.

▶ Small birds, such as this greenfinch, have a bouncing, undulating flight. To rest between flaps, they fold their wings against their body and glide for a short distance.

▶ A barn owl has large wings and a lightweight body. This allows it to fly very slowly and hover in the air with very little effort, helping it to spot prey on the ground below.

345

# Bird behavior

**The way a bird moves** can offer valuable clues that may help you to identify it. Birds may walk, hop, run, climb, swim, dive, or wade.

**Treecreepers and nuthatches** are usually seen climbing the trunks and branches of trees, while flycatchers sit on a perch and dart out to catch flying insects.

**Wagtails often patrol up and down** in the mud or short grass, wagging their tails up and down. Sometimes they make a dash after a passing insect.

**To warn another male** to keep out of his territory, a male great tit spreads his wings, shows off his black chest stripe, and turns his head from side to side to display his white cheek patches.

**Sparrows move on the ground** in short hops and feed in noisy groups. Dunnocks creep or shuffle slowly and quietly along the ground, on their own or in pairs, sometimes fluttering their wings.

**Birds that migrate**, such as swallows or house martins, often gather in large, noisy flocks before they set off on their migration journeys.

◀ *An adult great tit threatens a chaffinch with a noisy display.*

▲ *In spring, at dawn or dusk, the male American woodcock performs a spectacular display flight. It spirals high into the air, circles around, and then zigzags back to the ground, calling as it does so.*

**Gannets dive into the sea** from great heights with their wings half closed. This behavior is very obvious even from a long way away.

**Swans are very aggressive birds.** They defend their young fiercely by hissing and flapping their wings.

**Dabbling ducks**, such as mallards and teals, feed from the surface of the water, while diving ducks, such as tufted ducks, dive underwater to find food.

**Many male birds** display their colorful feathers to attract a mate. They may also give the female a gift of food, or show off their flying, or singing skills.

347

# Bird plumage

◀ A ptarmigan changes its plumage so it is camouflaged in all seasons. In winter its plumage is completely white, while in the summer its feathers are a mottled brownish-gray color.

**Winter plumage**　　**Summer plumage**

- **A bird's feathers** are called its plumage. They make up 4–12 percent of a bird's body weight.

- **Feathers grow inside thin tubes** called feather sheaths. As the feather emerges from the tip of the growing sheath, it unrolls and splits apart to form a flat blade. Eventually, the feather sheath itself splits open and flakes away.

- **Fully-grown feathers** are dead structures because their blood supply is cut off once they are fully formed. They become hollow and light.

- **At least once a year**, birds molt (shed) their old feathers, while new ones grow to take their place.

DID YOU KNOW?
In one day, a duck's wing feathers may grow the length of your little fingernail—or even more!

- **Molting allows birds** to replace worn or damaged feathers, which helps them to survive the winter or a long migration flight.

- **To help them identify birds**, birdwatchers need to know how their plumage changes when they molt their feathers, when the seasons change, or when juveniles mature into adults.

- **A bird never molts** all of its feathers at once. It keeps enough feathers at any one time to control its body temperature and keep itself dry and warm.

- **Small songbirds** take about five weeks to molt, while starlings take about three months.

- **Molting is a dangerous time** for ducks because they cannot fly while their new wing feathers are growing. They tend to hide away at this time.

- **Ducks molt** all their feathers and grow a new set of plumage in just a few weeks.

▶ *A king penguin with its adult plumage showing through some of the downy feathers that kept it warm as a chick. When a bird has grown all its adult feathers, it is said to have "fledged."*

# Looking after feathers

- **Birds must take great care** of their feathers to keep them clean and in good condition for flight. This is called preening.

- **Preening removes dirt** and parasites, such as feather lice and mites, which live on feathers and eat them away.

- **The way birds look after** their feathers is an important part of their behavior, which helps scientists to find out more about bird ecology and survival.

- **Jays sometimes** lie on the ground with their wings spread so that ants will crawl over them. The ants produce poisonous formic acid and this may help to get rid of parasites on the feathers.

- **Special feathers** called "powder down" feathers, which are found on a heron's breast and rump, crumble into a powdery substance. The bird rubs this into its plumage to remove dirt and fish slime.

- **The powder down feathers** of egrets, herons, and some other birds never stop growing, unlike ordinary feathers.

▶ *A pelican preening its feathers by drawing each one carefully through its bill.*

▶ *Some birds sunbathe, which may help them to absorb the sun's warmth on cold days, or perhaps repair their feathers on hot days.*

**During preening**, a bird collects preen oil from a gland under its tail and spreads this oil over its feathers. The oil probably helps to waterproof feathers and keep them in good condition, but it also kills bacteria and fungi.

**Many birds bathe in water** in order to clean and repair their feathers and get ready for preening. They flick the water over themselves with their wings, and raise and lower their feathers to allow the water to wash their skin.

**Many birds, such as house sparrows**, take regular dust baths. The gritty dust helps to rub dirt from their feathers.

▶ *In gardens, it is useful to provide birds with water all year round for drinking and bathing.*

# Tracks and signs

- **Even when** there is not a single bird to be seen, the tracks and feeding signs they leave behind provide valuable clues to their behavior, numbers, and diet.

- **Bird tracks in wet mud** or damp ground can be preserved by making a cast using plaster of paris.

- **Swimming birds**, such as ducks, leave webbed footprints, and wading birds leave tracks with long, slim toes spread wide apart. Perching birds leave tracks with a long first toe behind three long front toes.

- **When they land in snow**, birds leave a wing print, which is made by the long feathers of their wings.

- **Molted feathers** are fairly easy to find, even in towns. Feathers may also be left behind when a bird of prey plucks and discards them from its prey before eating.

- **Finches can crack open nuts** with their strong bills. They do not leave any bill marks on the two halves of the nut.

▶ These bird tracks in the snow are probably those of a perching bird. The three long toes that face forward are especially clear.

▲ *Bird pellets, such as these owl pellets, contain the remains of food that the bird cannot digest, such as bones, fur, or feathers.*

- **Nuts opened by birds** such as woodpeckers or nuthatches are usually wedged into cracks in tree bark.

- **Crossbills open pine cones** neatly with their curved bill to reach the seeds inside, whereas woodpeckers tear at the cones, making them look very messy.

- **Pellets are produced** by more than 300 species of bird, including birds of prey, gulls, and crows.

- **Green or brown goose droppings** can often be seen in parks. They are made of plant material and are about 2–3 in long.

# Farm birds

- **Ducks have been domesticated** for more than 2,000 years for their meat and eggs.

- **Originally from Africa**, the helmeted guineafowl was domesticated in Europe more than 2,500 years ago.

- **Domestic chickens** are descended from the red junglefowl, which was first domesticated 5,000 years ago. The junglefowl still lives wild in Southeast Asia.

- **Greylag geese** are the ancestors of most farmyard geese of today.

- **Sacred flocks of domesticated geese** occupied ancient Greek and Roman temples.

- **Domesticated geese range in size** from the big, white Embden ganders (adult males), which weigh 30 lb, to the tiny Egyptian goose, weighing a mere 4.8 lb.

- **Over 50 billion chickens** are reared every year for meat and eggs.

- **On factory farms**, chickens are kept in cages. Artificial lighting causes the birds to lay eggs all year round. Cage-free chickens are allowed to roam freely outside in more humane conditions.

- **The average egg weight** of the Japanese quail is about 10 percent of the hen's body weight.

- **Emus and ostriches** are raised on farms for their lean red meat. Their skin is tanned to make leather, their feathers are used in fashion and crafts, and their fat is turned into oil for health and beauty products.

▶ *Free range chickens are allowed to follow their natural behavior by pecking and scratching at the ground outside in search of food.*

DID YOU KNOW?
Some hens can produce
over 300 eggs a year.

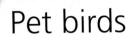

# Pet birds

▶ *African gray parrots are intelligent and affectionate, but can become bored and destructive if they do not receive enough attention.*

- **As early as 400 BC,** a Greek author wrote of owning a pet parrot—a bird that could speak words in both Indian and Greek!

- **Canaries were first domesticated** in the early 16th century. They are native to the Canary Islands, the Azores, and Madeira.

- **Siskins and goldfinches** have long been popular as cage birds, and are now rare in many areas.

- **When buying a pet bird,** take care to avoid buying a bird caught in the wild, and make sure you have prepared a suitable home and bought the correct food.

- **African gray parrots** live on average for 50 years, but can live for up to 75 years. They quickly learn to mimic sounds, such as the telephone ringing, and can copy and repeat the sound of the human voice.

- **Some birds**, such as cockatiels and doves, produce a lot of feather dust, which can cause allergies.

- **Finches and canaries** do not like being handled very much by their owners.

- **There are more than 70** different color patterns in pet budgerigars. An adult male budgie has a blue cere (small area that is bare of feathers) above its beak, while the female has a brown cere.

- **A budgie needs a cuttlefish "bone"** in its cage to provide it with calcium. It can also trim its bill on the cuttlefish.

- **It may take many weeks** or months to teach a budgie to talk, but some of these birds have learned hundreds of words or phrases.

▶ *A pet budgerigar uses its strong bill to crack open seeds, just as it does in the wild. Wild budgerigars are always green, but pet budgerigars have been bred in all sorts of color combinations.*

# Threats to birds

- **The main threats** affecting bird numbers are agriculture, logging, and the introduction of invasive species. The spread of agriculture significantly affects 73 percent of threatened bird species.

- **The Stephen Island wren** was named for the small island in Cook Strait, between the North and South Islands of New Zealand, where it lived. It is extinct, and some evidence suggests that it was killed off by a cat that belonged to the island's lighthouse keeper. It may have been the only flightless songbird.

- **The white feathers** of the great egret were popular decorations for hats in the late 1800s—more than 200,000 birds were killed for their feathers in a single year.

- **During the 19th century**, the wood duck was hunted nearly to extinction. The male's colorful feathers were used as ornate fishing flies and hat decorations.

◀ Seabirds may become covered in oil if an oil tanker is wrecked at sea or an oil rig is damaged. Sometimes they can be cleaned and released in an area of clean seawater, but often the oil is too thick for them to survive.

- **Many albatrosses** are dragged underwater and drowned when they try to feed on the baited hooks from longline fishing boats. About 18 out of 22 species of albatross are threatened with extinction.

- **Philippine eagles** are critically endangered due to deforestation caused by logging and clearance of forests for agriculture. Mining, pollution, pesticides, and poaching are also major threats to this magnificent bird. There are probably only 180–500 left in the wild.

- **The huia of New Zealand** was hunted for its feathers and also by European collectors. Its numbers were also reduced by introduced predators, such as rats, stoats, cats, and dogs. It is now extinct.

- **The campo miner** of the South American grasslands is now a vulnerable species since its habitat has been taken over by farms, cattle ranches, and plantations of non-native trees.

- **When mosquitoes** were accidentally introduced to the Hawaiian Islands in 1826, they devastated the birds on the islands by transmitting diseases such as bird small pox and bird malaria.

- **Numbers of house sparrows** have declined by more than 50 percent in the last 25 years, especially in urban and suburban habitats in many European cities. This may be due to an increase in predators and the use of more garden pesticides. Home improvements have also reduced the number of nesting sites in older buildings.

# Endangered birds

- **Over 1,200 (one in eight) birds** are threatened with extinction and 190 bird species are critically endangered, which means they face a very high risk of extinction in the near future.

- **Some bird families** are especially endangered, such as 82 percent of albatrosses, 60 percent of cranes, 27 percent of parrots, 23 percent of pheasants, and 20 percent of pigeons.

- **Endangered birds** live all over the world, but large numbers occur in tropical areas, especially in forests. Almost half of the world's endangered bird species live on islands. Island birds are very specialized and are not well adapted to deal with human threats.

- **The population of Algerian nuthatches** is less than 2,000 pairs. This species is threatened by fire, grazing, and tree felling, which have destroyed its habitat.

◀ *The Indian, or long-billed, vulture is one of the 20 most endangered birds in the world. It may be saved from extinction by being bred in captivity and released into the wild, although vultures have a long lifespan and breed slowly, so this will take a long time.*

- **Five vultures** that were common throughout India now face extinction, mainly as a result of being poisoned by a painkilling drug in the livestock carcasses they feed on. Since 1992, white-rumped vulture populations have declined by 99 percent.

- **The only wild population** of whooping cranes exists in Wood Buffalo National Park in Canada, where there were 266 birds in 2007, with 65 active nests.

- **Yellow-eyed penguins** live only in New Zealand and may be the rarest penguins in the world. About 4,000–5,000 individuals remain, but their numbers have been dramatically reduced by the destruction of their habitat, as well as introduced predators.

- **White-headed ducks** are one of the rarest birds in the world. Their survival is threatened by the drainage of their wetland habitat and its conversion to agricultural land. A population of 100,000 birds in the early 20th century has been reduced by nearly 80 percent to only 15,000 birds today.

- **The gorgeted puffleg** (a hummingbird) lives only in a small area of cloud forest in southwest Columbia, but about 8 percent of its habitat is being destroyed every year and replaced with coca plantations.

- **Less than 100 breeding pairs** of Madagascar fish eagles are left in the wild. Its wetland habitat has been polluted and destroyed to make way for rice fields. It is also persecuted because it competes for fish with people and is hunted for its body parts, which are used in traditional medicines.

# Bird conservation

- **Numbers of the Mauritius fody** have increased as a result of the work of the Mauritian Wildlife Foundation, which has tackled the threats of habitat destruction and invasive species.

- **Conservation measures** in Brazil have led to a four-fold increase in the numbers of Lear's macaws.

- **Various measures** are being taken to prevent longline fishing hooks killing at least 300,000 seabirds every year. These include using devices to scare birds, setting the lines underwater or at night, dying the bait blue, and weighting the lines so they sink underwater more quickly.

- **Spix's macaw** is probably extinct in the wild, but they are being bred in captivity at the Al Wabra Wildlife Preservation Center in the Arabian Gulf State of Qatar. It is hoped that some of these birds can eventually be reintroduced into their natural habitat in northern Brazil.

- **Numbers of the Chatham Island pigeon** have increased from 40 to about 200 due to predator and hunting controls.

- **Whooping crane numbers** have increased due to conservation measures that include using ultralight aircraft to teach birds bred in captivity where to fly on migration.

- **The population** of Hawaiian geese has increased from 30 birds in the mid 1900s to over 1,700 in 2006. However, most of the birds do not breed successfully in the wild—numbers are maintained by the regular release of captive-bred birds into the wild.

- **Conservation measures** to protect yellow-eyed penguins include the protection of key habitats, the removal of predators, and the use of nest boxes to provide shelter and protect the penguins from the heat of the sun.

- **The rare spoon-billed sandpiper** has been protected in its breeding, migration, and wintering areas in Russia, China, Hong Kong, Taiwan, India, and Vietnam.

▼ *The black robin, from the Chatham Islands off the coast of New Zealand, has been saved from extinction by using another species as a foster parent to sit on its eggs and rear some of its young.*

# Feeding the birds

🐦 **Putting out food** for wild birds on a regular basis reduces the amount of energy they have to spend searching for food. This can be important in cold weather or when the birds have young to feed in the summer.

🐦 **A bird such as a robin** can burn up one tenth of its body weight just staying alive during a cold night in winter.

🐦 **Putting out a wide range of food**, such as seeds, nuts, cheese, dried fruit, fresh fruit, and kitchen scraps will help birds to survive, and also allow you to watch them at close quarters.

🐦 **One way to feed birds** is to put food on a bird table, which can be just a simple tray fixed to a post or suspended from a tree.

🐦 **Try making a feeding bell**—any small bell or cup-shaped object filled with fat, cheese, or food mix. Hang it with the open end facing downward so that birds can cling underneath to feed.

🐦 **Hanging half a coconut from a tree** is a simple way to feed birds that can cling to the rim and feed on the nutritious white coconut inside.

▶ A roof on a bird table will help to keep rain, snow, and falling leaves off the feeding tray, and a raised edge will stop the food from falling off.

| 1 Collared dove | 6 Chaffinch | 11 Nuthatch |
| 2 Robin | 7 Blackbird | 12 Great tit |
| 3 Marsh tit | 8 Common starling | 13 Coal tit |
| 4 House sparrow | 9 Siskin | 14 Blue tit |
| 5 Brambling | 10 Great spotted woodpecker | 15 Greenfinch |

**Some birds, such as song thrushes**, prefer to feed on the ground, so food needs to be scattered on the yard or path. Keep the food away from plants or bushes where cats may leap out to catch the birds.

**Nestlings can choke on some foods**, such as nuts and dry bread. However, some birds give their nestlings a different diet from their own, such as protein-rich insects, which help them to grow.

**It is a good idea** to move a bird feeding site once or twice during the winter to avoid the risk of disease or infection. Bird feeders and bird tables should also be cleaned regularly for the same reason.

**Yards are good** for birds that eat ants and worms. So are many garden plants, especially those with berries such as hawthorn, rowan, holly, and yew. The seeds of plants such as sunflowers, scabious, thistle, dandelion, teasel, and nettle also provide good food sources for birds.

365

# Places to nest

🌿 **A nest box** provides an ideal opportunity to watch birds, but do not disturb them by looking inside the box.

🌿 **Nest boxes should be placed** out of direct sunlight and sheltered from the wind. They should have sloping lids so the rain runs off.

🌿 **The lid** needs to have a hinge so that the nest box can be cleaned easily. When the nestlings have left the box, open it out, take out the old nest, and clean the box thoroughly to prevent the spread of disease.

🌿 **A nest box** should be at least 6.5–10 ft above the ground, beyond the reach of cats.

🌿 **A box with a small round hole** about 30 mm across keeps out large birds and is ideal for woodland species, such as tits and nuthatches. A metal plate around the hole will stop woodpeckers or squirrels making the hole larger.

🌿 **Robins, flycatchers, wrens, and wagtails** prefer nest boxes with open fronts so that they can see out when they are sitting on their eggs.

🌿 **A perching post** in front of a nest box helps birds to land and take off, although it can encourage predators.

◀ As more and more wild habitats disappear, nest boxes in gardens and parks provide valuable homes for wild birds.

▲ Dead and decaying trees provide useful nesting and roosting sites for birds such as owls and woodpeckers.

🦉 **If the nest box** is a small log, the birds can cling to the rough bark instead of a perching post. Halve the log and hollow it out, drill a hole in one half, and nail the halves back together. Add a piece of wood for the roof.

🦉 **Treecreepers will sometimes use** nest boxes with side entrances, and tawny owls may nest in a long box rather like a chimney, placed at an angle of more than 45° to the horizontal.

# Index

# Index

Entries in **bold** refer to main subject entries.

# Acknowledgments

All artwork is from the Miles Kelly Artwork Bank

The publishers would like to thank the following sources for the use of their photographs:

Front cover Frans Lanting/FLPA

Back cover (c) Mircea Bezergheanu/Shutterstock.com, (b) Mogens Trolle/Shutterstock.com

Pages 10–11 Gail Johnson/Fotolia.com; 25(b) Robert Weber/iStockphoto.com; 40 Tui De Roy/ Minden Pictures/FLPA; 41 Geoff Moon/FLPA; 44–45 Kwest/Fotolia.com; 46 Konrad Wothe/Minden Pictures/FLPA; 47 Kaido Kärne/Fotolia.com; 48 Gertjan Hooijer/iStockphoto.com; 48 Gertjan Hooijer/iStockphoto.com; 53 Simon Litten/FLPA; 55 Frans Lanting/FLPA; 57 Yuri Timofeyev/ Fotolia.com; 60 Maria Bedacht/Fotolia.com; 63 Richard Lindie/iStockphoto.com; 66 Klavina/ Fotolia.com; 68 Scott Hudson/Fotolia.com; 72 Fotolia; 78 steve estvanik/Fotolia.com; 81 Mike Lane/FLPA; 82 JohnPitcher/iStockphoto.com; 83 Desmond Dugan/FLPA; 85 Paul Hobson/FLPA; 90 Jim Brandenburg/Minden Pictures/FLPA; 92 javarman/Fotolia.com; 96 David Hosking/FLPA; 100 David Thyberg/Fotolia.com; 101 jerome whittingham/iStockphoto.com; 105 David Hosking/ FLPA; 107 Martin Cleveland/iStockphoto.com; 108–109 Gertjan Hooijer/iStockphoto.com; 111 Sergey/Fotolia.com; 142 marilyn barbone/Fotolia.com; 143 Richard L. Carlson/Fotolia.com; 145 Neil Bowman/FLPA; 147 John Anderson/Fotolia.com; 150 ImageBroker/Imagebroker/ FLPA; 153 Phyllis/Fotolia.com; 156 Thomas Marent/Minden Pictures/FLPA; 161 Tomasz Kubis/ Fotolia.com; 163 Frans Lanting/FLPA; 165 Brian Lambert/Fotolia.com; 166 Andrew Howe/ iStockphoto.com; 169 suerob/Fotolia.com; 171 Marshall Folk/Fotolia.com; 173 Martin B Withers/ FLPA; 174 GCPabloImages/Fotolia.com; 180 DirkR/Fotolia.com; 181 Kerioak/Fotolia.com; 188 gregg williams/Fotolia.com; 193 Nikolay.Stoilov/Fotolia.com; 199 John Holmes/FLPA; 207 Gary K Smith/ FLPA; 208 ImageBroker/Imagebroker/FLPA; 224 Paul Tessier/iStockphoto.com; 233 Andrew Howe/ iStockphoto.com; 237 Andrew Howe/iStockphoto.com; 239 Tersina Shieh/Fotolia.com; 252 Liz Leyden/iStockphoto.com; 267 Steve Byland/Fotolia.com; 268 keller/Fotolia.com; 272 John Anderson/Fotolia.com; 273 Nicola Gavin/Fotolia.com; 283 Andrew Howe/iStockphoto.com; 292 Roger Tidman/FLPA; 297 RainforestAustralia/iStockphoto.com; 300–301 Gail Johnson/ Fotolia.com; 314 Fotolia; 321 EcoView; 330–331 John Anderson/iStockphoto.com; 338 Shawn P. Carey (Migration Productions); 340 John Daniels/ardea.com; 342 Andy Gehrig/iStockphoto.com; 345 (c) Andrew Howe/iStockphoto.com, (b) Nick Cook/iStockphoto.com; 346 Maurice Walker/ FLPA; 347 Steve Byland/Fotolia.com; 349 Erlend Kvalsvik/iStockphoto.com; 349 Erlend Kvalsvik/ iStockphoto.com; 351(t) michael luckett/Fotolia.com, (b) Frank Leung/iStockphoto.com; 352 Sandra van der Steen/Fotolia.com; 353 Kayleigh Allen; 355 Colin Monteath/Minden Pictures/ FLPA; 356 fivespots/Fotolia.com; 357 Raul Arrebola/Fotolia.com; 358 Mitsuaki Iwago/Minden Pictures/FLPA; 363 Geoff Moon/FLPA; 366 Noah Strycker/Fotolia.com; 368–369 John Pitcher/ iStockphoto.com

All other photographs are from:
Corel, digitalSTOCK, digitalvision, Image State, John Foxx, PhotoDisc

Every effort has been made to acknowledge the source and copyright holder of each picture. Miles Kelly Publishing apologizes for any unintentional errors or omissions.

# MINI ENCYCLOPEDIA
# BIRDS

## Mini book...
## masses of knowledge.

Crammed with information
flight, camouflage, eggs, migr
sounds, food, senses, nests, co          bitats,
identification, conservation, an   much more.

• Detailed guide to a huge range of bird species
• Hundreds of illustrations and photographs
• Amazing fact panels

BG - Juvenile
**ISBN 978-1-4351-5639-5**

50598

9 781435 156395

Manufactured in China

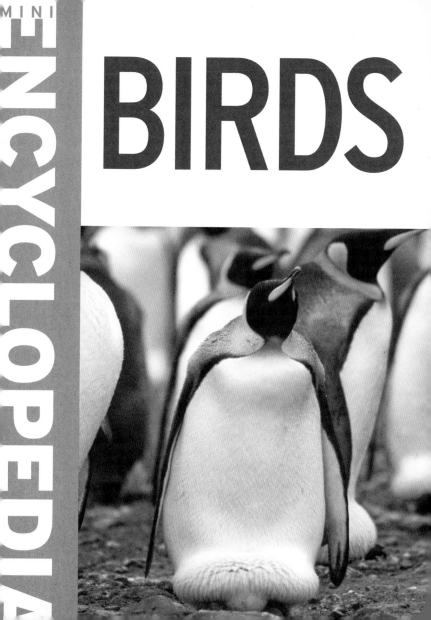

MINI

ENCYCLOPEDIA

# BIRDS

# THEY SPUN INTO SPIRAL!

# THEY GOT CLOSER!

# THEY FELL FOR FREEFALL!

# THEY DUG DEEPER!

# THEY DUG TUNNELS!

## COMING SOON!
# TERMINAL

RAL

RODERICK
GORDON

BRIAN
WILLIAMS

Chicken House
SCHOLASTIC INC.

Song lyrics from "Let's Panic Later" by Wire © 1979 ■ *The Book of Proliferation.*
English translation © 2000 Professor Grady Tripp, used with his kind permission.
■ Song lyrics from "The Son of God Goes Forth To War" by Reginald Heber (1812)
■ Song lyrics from "Time Is on My Side" by Jerry Ragovy © 1963, as later recorded by the Rolling Stones in 1964

ISBN 978-0-545-43027-2

12 11 10 9 8 7 6 5 4 3 2 1          13 14 15 16 17 18/0

Printed in the U.S.A. 40
First Scholastic paperback printing, November 2013

The text type was set in Vendetta.
The display type was set in Squarehouse.
Interior book design by Kevin Callahan